Freedom Code Writers:

Empowering Pathways to Promote Diversity and Inclusion in Computer Science Education

Unlocking Opportunities for Underrepresented Students to Thrive in the World of Code

Jordan B. Smith Jr., Ed.D.

Table of Contents

INTRODUCTION 1

CHAPTER 1: UNDERSTANDING THE OPPORTUNITY 3
THE REAL SITUATION OF UNDERREPRESENTED GROUPS IN COMPUTER SCIENCE 3
GENDER DIVERSITY 3
WHY AREN'T COMPUTER SCIENCE CLASSES MORE DIVERSE? 5
LACK OF AVAILABLE K-12 RESOURCES 6
LACK OF RESOURCES OUTSIDE THE CLASSROOM 7
DECLINE IN FEMALE PARTICIPATION 8
LACK OF POSITIVE ROLE MODELS 10
BENEFITS OF INCREASING DIVERSITY IN COMPUTER SCIENCE 14

CHAPTER 2: THE POWER OF REPRESENTATION 17
WHY STUDENTS NEED DIVERSE ROLE MODELS? 17
EXEMPLARY ROLE MODELS WHO OVERCAME BARRIERS 21
INTRODUCING POSITIVE ROLE MODELS TO YOUR CLASS 26

CHAPTER 3: RECRUITING GENDER MINORITIES TO COMPUTER SCIENCE CLASSES
.... 31
PROBLEMS FACED BY WOMEN AND GENDER MINORITIES 31
RECRUITING GENDER MINORITIES INTO COMPUTER SCIENCE 34
CREATING AN ALL-INCLUSIVE CLASSROOM FOR GENDER MINORITIES 36

CHAPTER 4: RECRUITING AFRICAN AMERICANS AND HISPANICS 41
OBSTACLES TO PURSUING DIGITAL AND IT CAREERS 41
RECRUITING TECHNIQUES TO INCREASE CLASSROOM DIVERSITY 46
INTRODUCING CULTURALLY RELEVANT RESOURCES INTO A CLASSROOM 50

CHAPTER 5: RECRUITING NATIVE AMERICANS TO COMPUTER SCIENCE CLASSES
.... 53
THE CHALLENGE OF INCREASING NATIVE AMERICAN REPRESENTATION IN COMPUTER SCIENCE
.... 53
SHOWCASING SUCCESSFUL NATIVE AMERICAN PROFESSIONALS 57
NETWORKING TO INCREASE NATIVE AMERICAN ENROLLMENT IN COMPUTER SCIENCE
EDUCATION 59
THE ROLE OF PARTNERSHIPS 64

CHAPTER 6: EMPOWERING ENGLISH LANGUAGE LEARNERS IN COMPUTER
SCIENCE EDUCATION 67

HOW ENGLISH LANGUAGE LEARNERS GET LEFT BEHIND 67
RESOURCES FOR YOUR ELL STUDENTS..71
BREAKING LANGUAGE BARRIERS IN COMPUTER SCIENCE.........................73
TEACHING STRATEGIES TO BOOST COMMUNICATION 75

CHAPTER 7: CREATING AN INCLUSIVE COMPUTER SCIENCE CURRICULUM 79

THE IMPORTANCE OF DIVERSE CURRICULA IN EDUCATION 79
CONSIDERATIONS FOR YOUR INCLUSIVE CURRICULUM 81
RESOURCES FOR BUILDING AN INCLUSIVE CURRICULUM 84
EXPLORING EXAMPLE CURRICULUMS 86

CHAPTER 8: BUILDING A SUPPORTIVE COMMUNITY AND PARTNERSHIPS...... 89

HOW COMMUNITY INVOLVEMENT CAN HELP ADDRESS UNDERREPRESENTATION IN COMPUTER SCIENCE EDUCATION..89
STRATEGIES FOR BUILDING EFFECTIVE COMMUNITY PARTNERSHIPS IN EDUCATION 91
LEVERAGING PARENTAL INVOLVEMENT FOR ENHANCED CLASSROOM SUCCESS 93
HOW PARTNERSHIPS DRIVE DIVERSITY IN COMPUTER SCIENCE........................95
P-TECH 98

CHAPTER 9: ADVANCED PLACEMENT, SCHOLARSHIPS, INTERNSHIPS, AND CAREER OPPORTUNITIES 101

HOW AP COURSES OPEN DOORS TO OPPORTUNITIES 101
WHAT TO EXPECT FROM AP COURSES 105
SCHOLARSHIPS FOR COMPUTER SCIENCE STUDENTS 108
INTERNSHIPS FOR COMPUTER SCIENCE STUDENTS 111
THE RANGE OF CAREERS AVAILABLE IN COMPUTER SCIENCE 113

CHAPTER 10: EMPOWERING STUDENTS TO MAKE A DIFFERENCE 121

HELPING UNDERREPRESENTED STUDENTS DEVELOP CONFIDENCE 121
EXAMPLES OF STUDENTS FIGHTING FOR CLASSROOM DIVERSITY 130
INSPIRING STUDENTS TO BECOME ADVOCATES FOR DIVERSITY 131

CHAPTER 11: EARNING COLLEGE CREDITS: AP COURSES AND CAL STATE SCHOOLS... 135

UNLOCKING THE VALUE OF ADVANCED PLACEMENT COURSES 135
AP COURSES AND CALIFORNIA STATE SCHOOLS 137
THE NEXT STEP TO CALIFORNIA STATE UNIVERSITY, LOS ANGELES (CAL STATE LA) 137
ADDITIONAL RESOURCES 139

CONCLUSION.. 143

ABOUT THE AUTHOR 145

GLOSSARY 149

REFERENCES 159

Introduction

What was the catalyst that led you to pick up Freedom Code Writers? Was it a nagging realization that the computer science world has yet to unlock its full potential due to a lack of diversity? Perhaps you were thinking of the countless talented and eager students who are overlooked simply because they don't fit the typical mold. Or maybe you, yourself, are one of those people. You know you have what it takes to revolutionize the industry, but you don't have the training you need to make it happen. The injustice weighs on your conscience, and you're determined to be a part of the change.

When you look at the leading figures in computer science and technology in 2023, who do you see? What do Bill Gates, Elon Musk, Mark Zuckerberg, and Jack Doresy have in common? They all come from the same cultural background. If a group of people from the same background, the same education, and the same life experiences face one problem, essentially they'll find only one route to solving the problem. You only need one person from a different walk of life to see new possibilities.

Why, you must wonder? Because when a group of individuals shares the same cultural background, the same educational path, and extremely similar life experiences, they tend to approach problems in much the same fashion. But invite in just one person from a different walk of life and they'll shatter those constraints, illuminate new avenues, and transform the entire problem-solving methodology.

You're here because you've felt the pangs of a predicament all too familiar to many. You're driven by a passion for computer science, yet you find yourself grappling with a dilemma. You understand the problems at hand, but the solutions seem elusive.

As you read this book, you'll gain insights and strategies to promote diversity and inclusion in computer science education, empowering you to tap into the immense potential that lies within diverse perspectives.

Imagine a world where computer science isn't confined to a select few, but thrives because of the contributions of individuals from all walks of life. Envision a future where innovation knows no boundaries, and breakthroughs emerge from the rich collection of human experiences. This is the world you're about to step into, guided by the knowledge within these pages.

Not so long ago, achieving equality seemed like an insurmountable challenge. Before the information you're about to learn became accessible, the path to change was difficult, dark, and treacherous. But here's the good news: Freedom Code Writers provides a beacon that lights your way toward a brighter, more inclusive future. Now, that might sound like a tall order, but as you move through this book, you'll find that it's not out of reach.

Freedom Code Writers is your guide, your ally, and your key to unlocking the potential of diversity in computer science. So let's embark on this educational journey together, and let the transformation begin.

Chapter 1:

Understanding the Opportunity

*Black and minority ethnic groups continue to be disadvantaged in higher education,
both for staff and students.*
–Kalwant Bhopal

In order to cover the degree of underrepresentation in computer
science and why this is such a problem for the both the industry and
the people affected, we need to identify misconceptions in computer
science classrooms and the many barriers students face.

The Real Situation of Underrepresented Groups in Computer Science

The field of computer science (CS) has long been under scrutiny for its
lack of racial and gender diversity. We'll begin our book by exploring
the findings of a study that compared the demographics of CS majors
at Stanford University in 2015 to those in 2020. We'll provide insights
into the progress made and the challenges that persist.

Gender Diversity

Historically, the tech industry has been male-dominated, and this trend
has naturally extended from academic programs. In 2015, the gender
breakdown among CS majors at Stanford was stark, with nearly 70%
being male and 30% female. The subsequent five years showed a
modest improvement, with women representing 34.4% of CS majors, a
4.4% increase since 2015.

This shift toward greater gender diversity is attributed to concerted efforts by the CS department. Initiatives like curriculum revisions, equity programs such as CS Pathfinders, and the support of student groups like Women in Computer Science (WiCS) have all contributed to this positive change. Nevertheless, the department acknowledges that more work is needed to achieve true gender parity (Andrews & Morris, 2020).

Race Diversity

In 2015, the racial breakdown of Stanford's CS students was as follows: 46.4% Asian, 38% white, 9.5% Latinx, and 6.1% Black. By 2020, the situation had evolved, but some disparities persisted. The Asian and white student populations continued to grow, while the representation of Black and Latinx students saw minimal change.

The percentage of Black and Latinx students in the CS department lagged behind their representation in the broader student population at Stanford. This suggests that, even though their numbers have increased slightly, these groups are still underrepresented in computer science.

Efforts are being made to address this disparity. The CS department is actively engaging with underrepresented minority student groups such as Black in CS to create a more supportive environment. Strategies include encouraging students to participate as section leaders, teaching assistants, and in CS research (Andrews & Morris, 2020).

Intersection of Gender and Race

When we consider the intersection of gender and race, we see that gender disparities persist within every racial category. In other words, the fraction of male students is larger than the fraction of female students no matter what their race. East Asian students have the best gender ratio, with approximately 54% men and 45% women. The Latinx category exhibits the largest gender disparity. Among Latinx students, female students make up less than a third of the population.

The majority of male CS students in 2020 were either white or East Asian, with white students comprising a slightly larger percentage (30.86% vs. 26.01%). The percentage of white male students decreased from 41% in 2015, while the percentage of East Asian male students remained relatively stable.

Among female CS majors, East Asian women are the most prevalent, with their representation staying consistent over the years. This indicates that even when categories are aggregated, the number of East Asian women clearly exceeds that of other groups.

The data from Stanford's CS department shows both progress and persistent challenges regarding diversity in computer science. Gender diversity has seen some improvement, thanks to dedicated efforts by the department and student groups. However, work remains to be done to achieve true gender parity.

When it comes to racial diversity, the representation of Black and Latinx students remains low compared to the broader student population, highlighting the need for continued efforts to promote inclusivity in computer science (Andrews & Morris, 2020).

This analysis is based on observed data because the university does not officially report race and gender statistics. Nevertheless, these trends underscore the importance of addressing diversity in computer science to create a more equitable and inclusive field for all aspiring technologists. While this is only one study, from one of the top-ranked CS schools in the US, we can extrapolate from this data the probable situation at other universities.

Why Aren't Computer Science Classes More Diverse?

Diversity is an important issue in computer science education, for reasons we will discuss in detail later. In order to improve the situation, we need to explore why we don't see more diversity. Several factors contribute to the lack of diversity in computer science classes, and understanding these challenges is the first step toward addressing them.

Lack of Available K-12 Resources

Access to quality computer science education at the K-12 level is a fundamental challenge that hinders diversity in the field. Let's take a look at the various factors at play.

Challenges in K-12 Computer Science Education

Many K-12 schools, particularly those in underserved communities, lack the necessary resources to offer comprehensive computer science courses. These resources include hardware and software, as well as qualified educators who can teach computer science effectively.

Even if schools have some access to technology, they may lack educators with the expertise to teach the classes. Computer science is a specialized field that is constantly changing, and not all K-12 teachers have the knowledge and skills to teach it. This lack of expertise can lead to a subpar educational experience for students. Even those who learn useful skills may find them outdated once they leave school.

Impact on Underrepresented Groups

The lack of resources in K-12 computer science education disproportionately affects underrepresented groups in several ways. Students from underprivileged backgrounds or attending schools with limited resources may miss out on the opportunity to explore computer science. This deprives them of exposure to a field that offers numerous career prospects and is critical for our increasingly digital world.

Without access to computer science education, many students may never discover their passion for technology and coding. This lack of exposure perpetuates stereotypes and reinforces the idea that computer science is not for them.

Lack of Resources Outside the Classroom

Access to technology and resources outside the classroom also plays an important role in shaping students' interest and proficiency in computer science. After all, one can only develop their skills to a limited extent at school. Not all students have equal access to computers and the internet at home, and that creates a significant barrier to diversity in the field. Let's take a look at the various factors at play.

The Digital Divide

The digital divide refers to the gap between people who have access to modern information and communication technology, including computers and the internet, and those who do not have access. This divide is particularly pronounced among underprivileged and rural communities, which often lack the resources necessary for students to engage with technology outside of school.

The Stanford study (Andrews & Morris, 2020) notes that only half of Black and Hispanic students have access to a computer at home. This statistic illustrates the stark disparities in technology access that exist along racial and socioeconomic lines.

Unequal access to technology outside the classroom can have a profound impact on students' preparedness for computer science courses. Students who lack access may not have the opportunity to practice coding, explore programming languages, or work on personal tech projects, putting them at a disadvantage.

Beyond preparedness, access to technology outside of school influences students' interest and engagement in computer science. Those who can explore technology at home are more likely to develop a passion for the field and pursue it academically and professionally.

Decline in Female Participation

The decline in female participation in computer science is a significant concern for the field's diversity and inclusivity. Historically, women were encouraged to enter computer science because of their typing skills, but this trend reversed as computing evolved. The history has created a perception that computer science is a male-dominated field, which discourages women from pursuing it. Let's take a look at the various factors at play.

Historical Context

In the early days of computing, specifically in the 1950s and the decades following, women played a significant role in the field. This era was marked by a more inclusive environment, largely because computing was still in its infancy, and the skills required for programming and data entry were seen as valuable, irrespective of gender.

Women such as Ada Lovelace, often regarded as the world's first programmer, and Grace Hopper, a pioneer in computer programming languages, made substantial contributions. During World War II, women like the ENIAC Six programmed one of the first electronic general-purpose computers. They were responsible for calculations that helped the war effort.

In these early years, programming involved a significant amount of data entry and calculations. Women's meticulous typing skills, honed from work as typists during the war, and their attention to detail made them well-suited for these roles. They became essential to the development of early computer systems.

However, as computing technology advanced, several significant changes occurred that contributed to the shift in the perception of the field.

Cultural Shifts

The post-World War II period witnessed significant cultural shifts, including a resurgence of traditional gender roles. This influenced the perception that programming and computing were more suitable for men, because woman should be home or doing more "feminine" jobs.

Marketing and Stereotyping

With the advent of personal computers in the 1970s and 1980s, marketing campaigns often targeted boys and men. This contributed to the perception of computing as a male-oriented activity. Movies and popular media began to depict programmers as socially awkward males, further reinforcing stereotypes.

Lack of Inclusivity

The emerging tech industry also struggled with creating inclusive environments. Male-dominated cultures developed within tech companies, which made it challenging for women to thrive in the field.

Education and Socialization

Young girls were subtly discouraged from pursuing interests in technology. Gendered toys, societal expectations, and a lack of female role models in computing all played a role in deterring women from entering the field.

The scarcity of female role models in computer science perpetuates the idea that it's not a welcoming space for women. When young girls and aspiring female computer scientists don't see women succeeding in the field, they can feel discouraged from pursuing careers in technology. This cycle creates a self-fulfilling prophecy, where the lack of representation leads to even fewer women entering the field.

Pay Gap and Lack of Inclusivity

The significant pay gap for women, Blacks, and Hispanics in STEM (science, technology, engineering, and math) fields, including computer science, is a substantial barrier to achieving diversity and inclusion in these sectors. Let's look at the various factors at play.

The Pay Gap in STEM

Research consistently shows that women and racial and ethnic minorities face substantial pay disparities in STEM fields, including computer science. They are often paid less than their male and non-minority counterparts for the same roles and responsibilities.

Several factors contribute to the pay gap and lack of inclusivity in STEM fields:

- Implicit bias and systemic discrimination can influence hiring, promotion, and salary decisions, leading to unequal compensation for women and underrepresented minorities.

- Women and minorities may face barriers to career advancement, limiting their access to higher-paying roles and leadership positions.

- The underrepresentation of women and minorities in leadership roles within STEM organizations can perpetuate the pay gap and lack of inclusivity.

- Research suggests that women are less likely to negotiate their salaries than men, which can contribute to disparities in pay.

Lack of Positive Role Models

The absence of a proportional number of role models from underrepresented groups in computer science is a significant barrier to achieving diversity and inclusion in the field. This lack of representation stands in contrast to other industries like entertainment, where diversity in leadership roles is on the rise. Let's take a look at the various factors at play.

Benefits of Positive Role Models

Positive role models from underrepresented groups serve as sources of inspiration and representation for aspiring individuals. They demonstrate that success is attainable, regardless of one's background. Kids can grow up saying, "I want to be like them."

Several factors contribute to the lack of positive role models from underrepresented groups, including:

- Historical lack of representation. Women and racial minorities have been marginalized and underrepresented in computer science, which has created a shortage of role models.

- Stereotypes and bias. Stereotypes and bias in the field may discourage individuals from underrepresented backgrounds from pursuing computer science careers.

- Lack of visibility. The achievements and contributions of underrepresented individuals in computer science are often overlooked or under-publicized, further diminishing their visibility as role models.

Language and Stereotypes

Language and stereotypes play a significant role in shaping the culture and environment of computer science, and their impact on diversity cannot be understated. Let's look at the factors at play.

Sexist Jokes and Gender-Based Bias

Sexist jokes and gender-based bias persist in the tech industry and, unfortunately, can extend into the recruitment process. These behaviors create a hostile and unwelcoming environment for women and underrepresented groups, discouraging them from pursuing careers in computer science. Examples of this bias include:

- Interview questions and bias. During technical interviews, some candidates may face biased or inappropriate questions. For example, female candidates might be asked about their family plans or personal life, which is not relevant to their technical qualifications. Interviewers may unconsciously exhibit bias by favoring male candidates or asking more challenging questions to female candidates, underestimating their abilities.

- Stereotyping in job descriptions. Job postings sometimes include gendered language that may unconsciously deter women from applying. For instance, using terms like "rockstar coder," "ninja developer," or "brogrammer culture" can make women feel like they don't belong.

- Gendered workplace culture. Sexist jokes and comments can be prevalent in tech workplaces, creating an uncomfortable atmosphere for women. This can include casual comments about women's appearance, abilities, or competence.

- Lack of representation in leadership. When women and underrepresented groups are underrepresented in leadership positions, the message is that these groups are not welcome or valued in the organization. This lack of representation can discourage women from pursuing careers in tech.

- Marginalization and isolation. Women and underrepresented groups may feel marginalized and isolated in male-dominated tech teams. This isolation can result from exclusionary behavior or the perception that they don't fit into the existing culture.

- Online Harassment and trolling. Female tech professionals, especially those in the public eye, often face online harassment, trolling, and threats based on their gender. This can deter women from entering or staying in the field.

Sexist jokes and gender bias contribute to a hostile environment where individuals from underrepresented groups may feel uncomfortable or unwelcome. This not only hinders their ability to thrive but also drives many talented individuals away from the field. Potential candidates, especially women and minorities, may be dissuaded from considering careers in computer science because of concerns about the culture they would be entering.

Male-Centric Language and Imagery

The language and imagery associated with computer science often reinforce a male-centric view of the field. This can be seen from course names to coding terminology to marketing imagery, among other places.

Course names such as Intro to Computer Science or Computer Engineering may seem gender neutral. However, "computer science" often implies a focus on the technical aspects, which may discourage individuals who do not identify as male. "Computer engineering" implies a focus on hardware and engineering, which may be perceived as more male-oriented.

Some coding terminology also can deter participation from underrepresented groups. "Master and slave" are used to describe the relationship between devices, where one controls the other. The use of such terminology can be seen as perpetuating power dynamics and gender hierarchies. In the context of Unix-like operating systems, "man pages" are documentation for various commands, even though they imply a male-oriented audience. "Bare metal," often used in embedded systems and low-level programming, can carry a connotation of toughness and masculinity.

Even the imagery in advertising and merchandise can perpetuate the stereotype of the male computer scientist or programmer. Historically, advertising for computers often features images of men working with computers, and merchandise such as t-shirts, stickers, and posters frequently use images or phrases that appeal to a male audience. Many tech-related conferences and events have mascots or icons that are male figures, such as Larry the Cucumber for the C programming language. Iconic figures like The Geek or The Nerd are typically portrayed as male, further contributing to the perception of computer science as a male-dominated field.

Coding comments or documentation commonly include gendered language like he or his when referring to a hypothetical developer, which can make female programmers feel excluded.

Benefits of Increasing Diversity in Computer Science

Diversity is not only a matter of social justice but also a driver of innovation and progress. Increasing diversity can yield numerous benefits that extend beyond the field itself. Let's explore six main advantages of greater diversity in computer science.

Equity and Inclusion

Diversity in computer science fosters equity and inclusion, allowing individuals from all backgrounds and identities to participate. An inclusive environment acknowledges the value of diverse perspectives, experiences, and talents. It ensures that everyone, regardless of their background, has an equal opportunity to pursue a computer science education and career.

Promoting equity and inclusion in computer science helps break down barriers that have historically excluded underrepresented groups. This, in turn, creates a more equitable society by providing pathways to economic prosperity and reducing social inequalities.

Creativity and Innovation

Diverse teams bring together individuals with varied viewpoints, problem-solving approaches, and life experiences. This diversity of thought and perspective is a catalyst for creativity and innovation. In computer science, innovation is driven by solving complex problems and developing novel solutions. Diverse teams are better equipped to tackle these challenges from different angles, leading to more creative and effective solutions.

When diverse minds collaborate, they bring unique insights to the table, sparking creativity and driving technological advancements. In computer science, innovation is essential for progress.

Skills

Diversity in computer science brings a wider range of skills and expertise to the table. Different backgrounds and experiences often translate into varied skill sets, such as language proficiency, cultural knowledge, and problem-solving abilities. These skills can be invaluable in addressing the complex and global challenges that computer scientists encounter.

By embracing diversity, computer science programs and organizations gain access to a more versatile talent pool. This diversity of skills can lead to more versatile and adaptable teams capable of addressing a broader range of problems and opportunities.

Positive Work Environment

A diverse and inclusive work environment is not only more equitable but also more enjoyable and satisfying for all employees. When individuals from diverse backgrounds feel valued and included, they are more likely to be engaged, productive, and motivated. A positive work environment fosters collaboration, trust, and a sense of belonging, which are essential for team success.

For computer science organizations and institutions, creating a positive work environment is a great way to attract and retain top talent. It also contributes to higher job satisfaction and lower turnover rates, reducing recruitment and training costs.

Environmental, Social, and Governance Agenda

Many companies and organizations are increasingly focused on environmental, social, and governance goals. Diversity and inclusion are integral components. Organizations that prioritize diversity align with societal values and demonstrate a commitment to ethical practices.

Bottom Line/Profitability

Research has shown that diversity can positively impact a company's bottom line and profitability. Diverse teams are better equipped to understand and cater to a diverse customer base, leading to improved products and services. Diverse organizations tend to be more innovative, which can lead to competitive advantages (Medium, 2023).

Diversity can directly impact the profitability of tech companies. A diverse workforce can help identify market opportunities, create products that resonate with diverse user groups, and expand the customer base.

In the next chapter, we will uncover the difference that a diverse class can have, and give examples of how some people from underrepresented groups have risen up and made significant changes.

Chapter 2:

The Power of Representation

*Educationists should build the capacities of the spirit of inquiry, creativity,
entrepreneurial and moral leadership among students and become their role model.*
–A. P. J. Abdul Kalam

Role models can inspire you, and you can use them to inspire your
classes as a teacher. So get ready to have any preconceptions you might
have blown away, just as these brilliant people have blown away the
preconceptions of their industry.

Why Students Need Diverse Role Models?

Diverse role models play an important role in shaping the aspirations
of your students. Dr. Alicia Nicki Washington, a distinguished figure in
computer science, exemplifies how positive role models can influence a
person's journey and foster diversity in the field. So, let's explore Dr.
Washington's story and its significance in the context of the need for
diverse role models.

Dr. Alicia Nicki Washington

Raised by parents who were strong advocates of education,
Washington's mother, a computer programmer at IBM, provided her
with access to technology and exposure to the world of computer
science from a young age. This early exposure naturally played a role in
sparking her interest in the field.

From assembling computers during her childhood to exploring
programming languages like BASIC and PASCAL by 10th grade,

Washington's journey was marked by a combination of access to resources and encouragement from her mother. Despite not initially intending to major in computer science, she continued to nurture her technical skills, leading to moments that would later shape her career.

Washington's decision to minor in computer science at Johnson C. Smith University marked a turning point in her life. In her C programming course, a perceptive professor recognized her natural aptitude for programming and encouraged her to change her major. This shift in trajectory highlights the importance of mentors and educators in recognizing and nurturing talent, especially among individuals who may not have initially considered certain fields.

Her pursuit of a Ph.D.—she was the first African American female to earn a Ph.D. in computer science at N.C. State University— demonstrates the transformative power of mentorship and support networks. The encouragement of her university president to apply for the David and Lucille Packard Fellowship paved the way for her career in research and academia.

Washington's story underscores the importance of diverse role models in computer science and STEM fields. Contrary to the belief that individuals have their career paths entirely figured out from the beginning, Washington's journey highlights the importance of seizing opportunities and taking chances. Her mother, a pioneering Black female programmer at IBM, not only shared her experiences but also instilled in her the value of reaching back and lifting others while climbing the ladder of success.

For many students, particularly those from underrepresented backgrounds, the presence of role models who look like them and have overcome similar challenges can be a source of inspiration and motivation. Washington's story exemplifies how a supportive family, mentorship, and a community of positive role models can pave the way for success in computer science (Washington, 2016).

The Need for More Diverse Role Models

Washington also highlights the unfortunate reality that not all students of color have access to the same level of role models and resources. The lack of role models who share their backgrounds and experiences, particularly for Black and Hispanic students, can make it difficult for these students to envision themselves in the field of computer science.

Washington's experience teaching a computer science course to a predominantly Black and Hispanic population of students in Washington, D.C., underscores the urgency of addressing this disparity. Many students couldn't name a computer scientist who looked like them. Diverse role models are essential for students to see reflections of themselves in both the curriculum and the educators guiding them (Washington, 2016).

Advancing Diversity in Computer Science

Dr. Alicia Nicki Washington's dedication to advancing diversity and inclusion in computer science led to her work on the K-12 CS Framework. Her work exemplifies her commitment to making computer science accessible to all students, regardless of their backgrounds. Her research and advocacy emphasize the importance of intentional efforts to prioritize diversity and inclusion in computer science education.

The Statistical Importance of Diverse Role Models

Statistics from a Gallup study, conducted in partnership with Amazon Future Engineer, provide concrete evidence of the positive impact of role models on students' interest in computer science careers. Let's examine this study in detail.

Role Models and Student Interest in Computer Science

The Gallup study, conducted in 2021, surveyed over 4,000 fifth-through 12th-grade students and found a strong correlation between the presence of role models in computer science and students' intentions to pursue such a career (Marken & Crabtree, 2021). Specifically, students who strongly agreed that they had a role model in computer science were more than 10 times as likely to express their plans to pursue a computer science career compared to those who strongly disagree (73% vs. 7%).

This striking difference shows the importance of role models in driving students' interest and future career choices in computer science.

The study also revealed that students' interest in computer science is closely tied to the presence of role models. Eighty percent of students who strongly or somewhat agree that they had a computer science role model expressed interest in learning about the topic. In contrast, only 43% of students who strongly or somewhat disagreed that they had a computer science role model expressed interest in learning about the subject.

These statistics show the impact that role models have on students' enthusiasm for computer science as a field of study.

Consistency Across Gender, Race, and Income

The positive influence of role models on computer science aspirations remained consistent across different demographic groups, including gender, race/ethnicity, and household income. This indicates that the benefits of role models are not confined to specific student populations, but are universal. These findings underline the broad significance of diverse role models in fostering diversity and inclusion in computer science.

However, the study also highlights challenges related to access to role models. Traditionally underserved populations, including rural students, Black students, and girls, reported having fewer role models in computer science.

Rural students, who often have limited access to computer science classes, were less likely to strongly agree that they have computer science role models (15% compared to 46% in large cities). Black students were the least likely to strongly agree that they have computer science role models. Girls were 10 percentage points less likely than boys to report having computer science role models (Marken & Crabtree, 2021).

These disparities in access to role models reflect broader inequities in computer science education and participation, particularly in rural areas and among historically underrepresented and marginalized students.

The statistics from the Amazon Future Engineer/Gallup Student Study unequivocally support the idea that role models are important in inspiring students' interest in computer science. Role models serve as mirrors, reflecting the possibilities and opportunities in the field, and windows, providing insights into the practical applications of computer science.

However, the study also highlights the existence of inequities in access to role models. These disparities align closely with differences in access to computer science education and participation. To foster diversity in the computer science workforce, more efforts are needed to provide all students with role models and a vision for a career in this in-demand field. Closing the gap in access to role models is a necessary step toward achieving greater diversity and inclusion in computer science, for the benefit of both the students and the industry as a whole.

Exemplary Role Models Who Overcame Barriers

Introducing students to exemplary role models will help to inspire and motivate them to pursue careers in computer science. With that in mind, let's look at some of the remarkable individuals who broke through barriers and left an indelible mark on the world of technology.

Alan Turing

Alan Turing was a brilliant mathematician and computer scientist who is celebrated for his groundbreaking work during World War II as one of the foremost code breakers. His efforts to crack the German Enigma code helped ensure an Allied victory. Turing is considered a visionary in the field of artificial intelligence (AI). He formulated the concept of the "Turing machine," a theoretical model of computation that laid the foundation for modern computer science.

However, Turing faced significant personal and societal challenges. Despite his immense contributions to science and technology, he was persecuted and criminally prosecuted for his homosexuality in a time when such relationships were criminalized. This persecution tragically overshadowed his legacy, and he died at a young age.

Turing's story serves as a poignant reminder of the importance of acknowledging and rectifying historical injustices, as well as the immense potential that can be stifled when prejudice and discrimination persist.

Lynn Conway

Lynn Conway is a trailblazing computer scientist known for her groundbreaking work in microchip design and VLSI (Very Large Scale Integration). She played a significant role in the development of technology that underpins modern computing devices.

However, Conway faced adversity in her career. She was fired from IBM in the 1960s when she revealed her intention to transition as a transgender woman. Despite this setback, she persevered and went on to achieve remarkable success in academia and the tech industry.

Conway serves as a testament to the resilience and determination required to overcome societal prejudice. Her advocacy for transgender rights and visibility in the tech industry has paved the way for greater inclusion.

Ada Lovelace

Ada Lovelace is widely recognized as the world's first computer scientist, living in the 19th century, an era when women were discouraged from pursuing education and careers in science and technology. She made significant contributions to Charles Babbage's analytical engine, a precursor to the modern computer. Lovelace's notes on the engine included what is considered the first computer program, earning her the title of the first programmer.

Lovelace's accomplishments are all the more remarkable considering the societal barriers and expectations placed on women in the 1800s. Her pioneering work laid the foundation for computer programming and serves as an inspiration for women and girls interested in technology.

Kimberly Bryant

Kimberly Bryant is an electrical engineer and tech entrepreneur who founded Black Girls Code, a nonprofit organization dedicated to empowering Black girls with computer science skills. Recognizing the lack of diversity in the tech industry, Bryant created a platform that provides STEM education and mentorship opportunities to underrepresented minorities.

Bryant's commitment to bridging the racial and gender gap in tech is a testament to her dedication to diversity and inclusion. Her work not only provides young girls with the technical skills needed in the digital age but also instills confidence and ambition, inspiring the next generation of diverse tech leaders.

Annie Jean Easley

Annie Jean Easley was a remarkable computer scientist, mathematician, and rocket scientist whose groundbreaking work at NASA helped shape the course of space exploration. Easley's 34-year career at NASA began in 1955. She eventually served as a team leader responsible for developing software for the Centaur rocket, an integral component of NASA's missions.

Easley's contributions to the field of computer science and her role at NASA are made all the more impressive considering the challenges she faced as one of the first African Americans to work at the agency during a time of racial segregation and discrimination. Her accomplishments broke down barriers and opened doors for future generations of African American scientists and engineers.

Kaya Thomas

Kaya Thomas is an American app developer and a passionate advocate for diversity in technology. She has made significant contributions to the tech industry through her work in developing mobile applications and her dedication to increasing diversity in STEM fields.

Thomas is particularly known for her role as a volunteer mentor with Black Girls Code, an organization dedicated to empowering Black girls with computer science skills. Her commitment to mentorship and her efforts to promote diversity have earned her recognition, including an honor from former first lady Michelle Obama.

Thomas exemplifies the importance of paying it forward by inspiring and supporting the next generation of diverse tech talent.

Philip Emeagwali

Philip Emeagwali is a mathematical genius and computing pioneer whose remarkable journey to success is an inspiration to many. Despite growing up in a family with limited resources and eight children, Emeagwali's pursuit of education led him to become the first African to work toward a Ph.D. in mathematics.

Emeagwali is perhaps best known for his work on the Connection Machine, which was recognized as the world's fastest computer at the time. His groundbreaking contributions to parallel processing and computational science have left an permanent mark on the field of computer science.

Emeagwali's story stresses the transformative power of education and determination. His achievements serve as a reminder that brilliance knows no boundaries and that anyone, regardless of their background, can make significant contributions to the world of technology.

Luis von Ahn

Luis von Ahn is a pioneering computer scientist known for his innovative contributions to the tech world. He is renowned as the inventor of reCAPTCHA, a widely used security tool that also helps digitize books and other printed materials. This ingenious solution harnesses human efforts to solve CAPTCHAs and has made a significant impact on both security and digital preservation.

Von Ahn's commitment to accessible education led him to co-create Duolingo, a popular language learning platform that offers free language courses to millions of users worldwide. His work has made learning new languages more accessible and affordable, opening up opportunities for people around the globe.

Von Ahn's story highlights the potential for technology to solve real-world problems and improve accessibility to education and information.

Victoria Chavez

Victoria Chavez is an inspiring computer scientist and developer who has dedicated her career to making computer science and educational technologies more accessible to students with disabilities. She developed the app SNAPy, which helps people with communication challenges express themselves using images and text.

Chavez is deeply committed to advocating for inclusive education technologies that empower students with disabilities to thrive in academic settings. Her efforts contribute to a more equitable and accessible education system for all.

Chavez demonstrates the power of using technology to address important social challenges and create positive change in the lives of individuals with disabilities.

Daniel Loreto

Daniel Loreto is a Venezuelan American computer scientist and tech leader whose career has spanned prestigious companies like Google, Twitter, and Airbnb. He earned his education at the Massachusetts Institute of Technology, where he honed his skills and knowledge in computer science.

Loreto showcases the opportunities that exist for individuals in the field of computer science to work at some of the most influential tech companies in the world. His achievements show the importance of education and expertise in achieving success in the tech industry.

Loreto serves as an inspiration to aspiring computer scientists, particularly those from underrepresented backgrounds, demonstrating that with dedication and talent, anyone can excel in the tech world.

Introducing Positive Role Models to Your Class

Introducing positive role models in the classroom is a great way to inspire and motivate students, helping them see the potential in themselves. By showcasing a diverse range of role models, both historical and contemporary, you can broaden students' perspectives and encourage them to pursue careers in computer science and other STEM fields. Let's examine some effective teaching strategies to introduce positive role models to your class.

Incorporate Historical Figures

Start by introducing students to influential historical figures who made significant contributions to computer science. For example, highlight pioneers like Ada Lovelace and Alan Turing. Inspire your students by sharing their stories, achievements, and the challenges they overcame.

Bring in Modern Celebrities and Community Members

Expand the definition of role models beyond historical figures. Discuss contemporary celebrities, scientists, and community members who have made notable contributions to technology and computer science. For instance, you can talk about Elon Musk's innovations in space and electric vehicles or Malala Yousafzai's advocacy for girls' education.

Share Personal Experiences

Be open with your students about your own journey in computer science. Share your passion for the subject and the challenges you faced. Let them see you as a role model who is actively engaged in the field and continuously learning. Your enthusiasm can be infectious—in a good way.

Engage Former Pupils

Invite former students who have pursued careers in computer science or STEM to speak to your current class. They can share their experiences, career paths, and the impact of their computer science education. Having relatable peer role models can be particularly inspiring.

Collaborate With Other Schools

Create collaborative projects or activities with students from other schools, especially those with diverse backgrounds and experiences. This allows your students to interact with peers from different communities and learn from one another. It can also expose them to new role models and perspectives.

Organize Motivational Speakers

Network within your professional community to identify potential guest speakers who can visit your class. Reach out to professionals, researchers, or entrepreneurs in computer science who can share their insights, experiences, and career journeys with your students.

Use Fictional Figures

While real-life role models are valuable, fictional characters from literature, movies, and television can also inspire students. Encourage discussions about the traits and values portrayed by these characters. For instance, Hermione Granger from the Harry Potter series is known for her intelligence and problem-solving skills.

Highlight Diversity

Emphasize the importance of diverse role models in computer science. Showcase individuals from different backgrounds, genders, ethnicities, and abilities. This helps students connect with role models who reflect their own identities and experiences.

Encourage Self-Reflection

Prompt students to reflect on what qualities they admire in role models and how they can use those qualities in their own lives. Encourage them to set personal goals and aspirations based on the inspiration they draw from role models.

Create Role Model Projects

Assign projects that require students to research and present about a role model of their choice. This allows them to delve deeper into the lives and contributions of inspiring figures and share their findings with the class.

Foster a Growth Mindset

Emphasize the importance of effort, resilience, and continuous learning. Teach students that they can aspire to be like their role models by developing their skills and working toward their goals.

Promote Positive Online Behavior

Discuss responsible and respectful online behavior with your students. Encourage them to follow and engage with role models on social media platforms to stay updated on their activities and achievements.

Now that we know why our classrooms need to be more diverse, it's time to get into techniques for putting the why into practice. In next chapter we will dive headfirst into these techniques. See you there!

Chapter 3:

Recruiting Gender Minorities to Computer Science Classes

"Both women and computer science are the losers when a geeky stereotype serves as an unnecessary gatekeeper to the profession."
–Cordelia Fine

The goal of this chapter is to give you a better understanding of why females and other gender minorities struggle to excel in computer science and how we can help them. This chapter also will cover LGBTQIA+ to ensure no minority group is excluded.

Problems Faced by Women and Gender Minorities

Despite the many opportunities that technology has provided, challenges faced by women and gender minorities are still quite prevalent. Some of the main problems they face include:

Lack of Representation

When women and gender minorities don't see themselves reflected in STEM fields, they can't imagine a place for themselves. The absence of role models who share their gender identity or sexual orientation leads to feelings of isolation and self-doubt.

Negative Stereotypes

Negative stereotypes surrounding women in computer science continue to persist. These stereotypes perpetuate the belief that women are less technically competent or less suited to technical roles than men. Such unfounded assumptions can discourage women from pursuing careers in technology and can even lead to self-fulfilling prophecies where they begin to doubt their own abilities.

Belongingness and Dropout Rates

The feeling of not belonging is a significant issue faced by women and gender minorities in computer science programs and in workplaces. This sense of exclusion can stem from a variety of sources, including the lack of representation, negative stereotypes, and gender discrimination. As a result, many women and gender minorities choose to leave programs or jobs where they do not feel valued or included, leading to higher dropout rates.

Gender Discrimination

Gender discrimination remains pervasive in computer science. Behaviors such as mansplaining (condescending explanations from men to women) and gaslighting (manipulation of information that causes causing self-doubt) can create hostile work environments. Reporting such behavior can be daunting for women and gender minorities, because they may fear backlash or a lack of support from their superiors.

Stereotype Threat

Stereotype threat is the fear of confirming negative stereotypes about one's group, which can lead to underperformance. In computer science, women and gender minorities may feel added pressure to prove themselves above and beyond their peers, causing stress that impacts their performance and overall well-being.

Unconscious Bias

Unconscious bias affects hiring, promotions, and everyday interactions. Biases can lead hiring managers to unconsciously favor candidates conforming to traditional gender roles, limiting opportunities for women and gender minorities. These biases also influence how individuals are treated in team settings, potentially hindering contributions to the field as well as career advancement.

Intersectionality

For those who belong to both the LGBTQIA+ community and other marginalized groups, such as women of color, challenges can be even more pronounced. They may face discrimination based, for example, on both their gender and sexual orientation, necessitating the simultaneous addressing of multiple layers of bias and discrimination.

Stereotype Perpetuation

The persistent belief that boys are better at computer science is a harmful stereotype that discourages young girls and gender minorities from pursuing interests in technology. This stereotype can also influence teachers and parents in guiding children away from these fields.

Lack of Inclusive Policies and Support

Many educational institutions and workplaces lack inclusive policies and support systems tailored to the needs of women and gender minorities. These could include mentorship programs, support groups, and training to combat gender bias.

Hostile Online Spaces

Women and gender minorities in tech may encounter hostility and harassment in online spaces, including social media and forums. This online abuse can deter them from participating in tech communities and exacerbate feelings of exclusion.

Recruiting Gender Minorities Into Computer Science

So how does one go about recruiting gender minorities? Diversity and inclusion foster innovation and solving complex problems, especially if those problems are prevalent and need a fresh perspective. Gender minorities have been historically underrepresented in computer science, even though many have contributed a great deal to the field over the years. To bridge this gap and create a more inclusive environment, organizations and educational institutions can implement the following strategies:

Be Vocal About Diversity Goals

Organizations should communicate their commitment to diversity openly. This means actively participating in events, conferences, and networking opportunities related to gender diversity in tech. Setting clear diversity goals and publicly announcing them shows that the company is serious about change rather than just using diversity for positive PR.

Inspire a New Generation

Partnering with schools and universities to promote STEM subjects as viable career options for young girls, and other gender minorities is a great way to increase their participation later in life. Female professionals in the field should visit schools, share their experiences, and serve as role models.

Remove Bias from Job Descriptions

Gender bias often begins with the language used in job descriptions. Companies should avoid using gender-related superlatives or adjectives that may alienate potential female candidates. They should ensure that job descriptions are neutral and inclusive in terms of language, and be cautious when translating job descriptions into languages with gendered nouns to avoid unintended bias.

It might be necessary reconsider the skill requirements listed in job descriptions. Research shows that women are less likely to apply for a job if they don't meet 100% of the listed skills. Organizations can distinguish between essential and nice-to-have skills to encourage more diverse applicants.

Actively Seek Female Talent

In their quest to attract more female applicants for technical roles, organizations should consider proactive sourcing. Directly reaching out to potential candidates showcases the value placed on their skills and experiences. They can also advertise that they are looking for people from diverse backgrounds.

Leveling the Interview Process

To create a welcoming environment for candidates, the organization should consider involving a diverse panel when conducting interviews. The presence of women and gender minorities in technical roles within the organization assures candidates that they won't be the sole member of their gender.

If assembling a diverse interview panel isn't feasible, the organization should ensure that the candidate pool itself is diverse. Offering candidates a glimpse of the company culture, such as showcasing the office or workspace, can dispel preconceived notions and create a more inclusive environment.

Offering Clear Progression Opportunities

Organizations should provide training and mentorship programs for all employees to advance in their careers. This reinforces the message that the organization cares about its employees, regardless of their gender. Promoting women into leadership positions should be based on their skills and accomplishments rather than merely fulfilling diversity quotas.

Promoting Equal Pay

Addressing the gender pay gap means ensuring that all employees, irrespective of gender, receive fair compensation. Employees should be paid based on their work, not their gender.

Offering Family-Friendly Benefits

People of all genders grapple with the challenge of balancing career and family. Organizations should provide family-friendly benefits. These may include parental leave, flexible working arrangements, and work-from-home options.

Creating an All-Inclusive Classroom for Gender Minorities

Diversity and inclusion in the workplace begin with education. Therefore, it is imperative that all classes are inclusive. You can do this in a few ways in your classroom.

Make Learning a Social Experience

Encouraging a sense of community and collaboration can aid in making the classroom more inclusive. Establish group projects and collaborative assignments that promote interaction among students. These activities can help break down barriers and create a supportive network within the classroom.

Try organizing extracurricular events, such as coding clubs or hackathons, where students can further engage with their peers. These events can provide opportunities for gender minorities to build confidence and form connections within the field that will help them after school.

Bridge the Confidence Gap

Many female and nonbinary students may doubt their abilities or feel intimidated by the perceived male-dominated culture of the field. You can bridge the gap through:

- Mentorship: Pairing gender minority students with mentors, whether they are professors, graduate students, or industry professionals, can boost their confidence and provide guidance.

- Supportive feedback: Create a classroom environment where constructive feedback is encouraged, and mistakes are viewed as opportunities for growth. Encourage students to share their ideas and celebrate their achievements, no matter how small.

- Visible role models: Highlight successful women and nonbinary individuals in computer science through guest lectures, profiles, or discussions. Seeing relatable role models can inspire students and boost their confidence.

Welcome Late Bloomers

Not all students enter computer science with prior experience or an early interest in the field. Some may discover their passion for technology later in their academic journey. This doesn't mean that they will be any less successful than their peers. You can welcome late bloomers through:

- Introductory courses: Offer introductory computer science courses that assume no prior knowledge. These courses should focus on building a strong foundation and demystifying the subject matter.

- Flexible learning paths: Provide flexible learning paths that allow students to catch up and progress at their own pace. Offer additional resources, such as online tutorials or workshops, for those who need extra support.

Nontraditional Students

Recognize that gender minorities come from diverse backgrounds. Accommodate nontraditional students who may have work or family commitments by offering evening classes or online options.

Use Real-World Examples

Connecting classroom material to real-world applications can make computer science more relatable and engaging for all students. Use examples and projects that demonstrate the practical relevance of the concepts being taught.

Case Studies

Use case studies that show how computer science is used to address real-world challenges, such as solving social issues or advancing medical research.

Guest Speakers

Invite guest speakers from various industries to share their experiences and describe how they apply computer science in their careers.

Hands-On Projects

Assign projects that require students to solve practical problems. Encourage them to collaborate with local organizations or nonprofits to work on projects that have a meaningful impact.

Make the Classroom Less "Geeky"

The perception of computer science as a "geeky" or exclusive field can deter some gender minorities from pursuing it. To make the classroom more welcoming, you can do the following:

- Diversify the curriculum: Offer a diverse curriculum that includes not only coding but also human-computer interaction, data ethics, and interdisciplinary courses that appeal to a wider range of interests.

- Use inclusive language: Use inclusive language in teaching materials and discussions. Avoid technical jargon that may alienate students who are new to the field.

- Create an inclusive environment: Ensure that the physical classroom and digital learning platforms are accessible and welcoming to all. Consider the needs of students with disabilities and provide resources for accessible learning.

The next group of underrepresented students that we will be exploring is African Americans. We will discover the unique challenges they face and explore how we can reduce these challenges in the next chapter. Catch you there!

Chapter 4:

Recruiting African Americans and Hispanics

You can absolutely be what you can't see! That's what innovators and disruptors do.
–Kimberly Bryant

The goal of this chapter is to help you to understand why African Americans are underrepresented, how to encourage more African Americans into the classroom, and how you can teach computer science in a culturally meaningful way.

Obstacles to Pursuing Digital and IT Careers

A survey of more than 1,000 Black Americans, conducted by AudienceNet, provides central insights into the obstacles that African Americans encounter when considering careers in digital and information technology. These obstacles reflect a complex interplay of factors, including social, economic, educational, and cultural elements. Let's dive into these elements next, so that we can understand their causes, effects, and remedies.

Lack of Knowledge and Awareness

A significant barrier to entry for Black Americans is the pervasive lack of knowledge and awareness regarding where to start when considering a career in computer science, with 55% of Black Americans surveyed feeling uncertain about the initial steps (AudienceNet, 2019). The root causes of this lack of awareness are the result of limited exposure to digital and IT career paths and insufficient access to information about available opportunities.

For many Black Americans, especially those from underprivileged backgrounds or underserved communities, exposure to digital and IT fields is often minimal. This lack of exposure can be attributed to several factors, including the absence of tech-related programs or extracurricular activities in their schools and neighborhoods. Without exposure to these fields, they may remain unaware of the potential career paths and opportunities that exist within digital and IT industries.

Even when some level of exposure exists, the lack of readily available and accessible information about digital and IT careers can be a major stumbling block. Access to comprehensive and accurate information about the educational requirements, job prospects, and potential career trajectories in these fields is needed. Without such guidance, individuals may find it daunting, and perhaps even impossible, to join the industry.

Skills Gap

Another significant barrier facing Black Americans interested in digital and IT careers is the skills gap. A considerable portion, 52%, of respondents expressed concerns about not possessing the right skills for these professions (AudienceNet, 2019). This issue is deeply rooted in disparities in educational resources and training opportunities, and access to quality instruction.

In many cases, Black students face disparities in educational resources and opportunities compared to their non-Black peers. Insufficient funding, overcrowded classrooms, and a lack of advanced coursework can hinder the development of the technical skills needed for digital and IT careers. This disparity in educational experiences can result in a deficiency in the fundamental technical competencies required for success in these industries.

Access to training programs and resources such as coding bootcamps or specialized technical courses is often constrained by financial and geographical factors. Many individuals, particularly those from disadvantaged backgrounds, may not have the financial means for or proximity to such programs. In the end, they miss out on opportunities to acquire the skills necessary to compete in the job market (AudienceNet, 2019).

Financial Barriers

Financial constraints represent another formidable obstacle for Black Americans aspiring to enter the field. In the AudienceNet survey, 51% of respondents cited financial reasons as a hindrance to pursuing careers in these sectors.

Pursuing a career in technology frequently requires investing in education and training. The costs associated with obtaining a relevant degree or certification can be exorbitant, making it financially prohibitive for many individuals and families. The burden of student loans or the need to work to support oneself or one's family can hinder the pursuit of education in these fields.

Financial barriers extend beyond tuition to include access to essential resources like computers, software, and high-speed internet. Inequities in access to these resources can further exacerbate the challenges faced by aspiring Black professionals.

Limited Network

The importance of networking cannot be overstated. Unfortunately, 44% of Black Americans reported not knowing anyone in the technology sector that they could consult or seek guidance from (AudienceNet, 2019). Networking is important for career advancement, providing opportunities for mentorship, job referrals, and professional growth. The absence of a supportive network is thus a substantial disadvantage. Black individuals who lack connections in the industry may find it more challenging to access job openings, stay informed about industry trends, or receive guidance on navigating career paths.

Perceived Exclusivity and Fit

According to the survey, nearly 38% of respondents expressed concerns about not fitting into the tech industry (AudienceNet, 2019). That feeling can be influenced by various factors such as a lack of diversity in the field, unconscious bias, or harmful stereotypes.

The underrepresentation of certain groups in the tech industry contributes to the perception of exclusivity. When potential candidates do not see people who look like them in tech roles, they may feel discouraged from pursuing such careers. Increasing diversity within tech companies and showcasing diverse role models can help dispel this perception (AudienceNet, 2019).

Unconscious bias and stereotypes can create an unwelcoming environment. Tech companies need to address these biases through awareness training, diversity, equity, and inclusion programs, and by actively challenging harmful stereotypes. This isn't just for the good of Black Americans, it's good for the company, too.

Access to Technology and Mentoring

Access to technology, training, and mentors is an important factor in skill development and career guidance. For Hispanic Americans, this represents one of the primary obstacles to entering the tech industry. Initiatives that offer subsidized or loaner equipment can help level the playing field for individuals who lack access to these resources.

Establishing mentorship programs that pair individuals with experienced professionals can provide valuable guidance and support. These mentors can offer insights into the industry and career advice, and help newcomers navigate the challenges of entering the tech world.

Educational Attainment

Achieving a diverse talent pool in tech requires addressing educational disparities. While 47% of AudienceNet survey respondents had obtained a postsecondary credential—41% in a STEM subject and 27% in computer science—a significant portion of the population lacks STEM backgrounds. The reasons for this include:

- Perceived difficulty: Efforts should be made to debunk myths about the difficulty of STEM subjects. Encouraging students from diverse backgrounds to pursue STEM education and providing them extra support and resources can help overcome this perception.

- Information accessibility: Making information about STEM and computer science education more accessible is extremely important. Providing clear pathways and information about scholarships, and showcasing success stories, can demystify the educational journey in these fields.

- Job satisfaction and advancement: While attracting diverse talent is one aspect, retaining and advancing that talent is equally important. Many respondents in digital and IT positions face challenges such as long working hours, dissatisfaction with compensation, and limited career advancement.

- Workplace equity: Tech companies should prioritize creating equitable workplaces. This includes addressing pay disparities, offering flexible work arrangements, and providing clear paths for career advancement and leadership opportunities.

- Employee support programs: Implement employee support programs that address mental health, work-life balance, and job satisfaction. Happy and well-supported employees are more likely to stay in the industry.

Recruiting Techniques to Increase Classroom Diversity

Diverse perspectives and backgrounds bring fresh ideas and innovation, which are vital for solving complex problems and creating inclusive technology solutions. However, achieving diversity in the computer science classroom and, ultimately, in the workforce, can be a challenging task. To overcome these challenges, educational institutions and educators must employ effective recruiting techniques tailored to increasing classroom diversity. So why don't we take a look at what recruitment methods you can use to attract more African Americans and Hispanics to your class? Many of these are similar or even the same as the ones we explored in the previous chapter.

Being Vocal About Diversity Goals

Transparency when recruiting students from underrepresented backgrounds will go a long way. Educational institutions should openly communicate their commitment to diversity and inclusion. They can do this through official statements, mission statements, and public awareness campaigns. When students and parents are aware of a school's dedication to diversity, they are more likely to consider the school as a viable option.

Creating a Welcoming Environment

Creating an inclusive and welcoming atmosphere will help in recruiting a diverse student body. Computer science departments should actively work on building a sense of belonging for students from all backgrounds. This includes implementing mentoring programs, support networks, and affinity groups where students can connect with peers who share similar experiences.

Resources for Educators of Hispanic and Latino Students

Now, let's focus on specific recruiting resources that you as an educator can use for Hispanic and Latino students:

STEM Transformation Institute

The STEM Transformation Institute is an excellent resource for educators and students interested in STEM fields. Schools can collaborate with this institute to create outreach programs, scholarships, or summer camps targeting Hispanic and Latino students.

Pathways to Student STEM Success

This initiative focuses on creating clear academic pathways for students interested in STEM fields. Schools can leverage this program to provide guidance and resources specifically designed for Hispanic and Latino students, helping them navigate the complexities of STEM education.

HSI-STEM

Hispanic-Serving Institutions (HSIs) are schools with a significant Hispanic and Latino student population. Schools aspiring to increase diversity can partner with HSIs to develop pipeline programs, articulation agreements, or dual-enrollment options that facilitate the transition of Hispanic and Latino students into computer science programs.

Queens STEM Academy

Schools can collaborate with institutions like the Queens STEM Academy to organize workshops, seminars, and exposure programs that introduce Hispanic and Latino students to the world of computer science. These initiatives can help demystify the field and spark interest among potential future students.

Project Raise

Project Raise, a program aimed at increasing diversity in STEM fields, offers a range of resources that schools can tap into. Educational institutions can access funding, mentorship opportunities, and curriculum support tailored to attracting and retaining Hispanic and Latino students.

Recruiting Resources for Black Students

As with Hispanic and Latino students, several resources are tailor made for Black Americans.

National Society of Blacks in Computing (NSBC)

NSBC is an organization dedicated to supporting and advancing Black professionals and students in the field of computing. Educational institutions can partner with NSBC to access a network of Black computer scientists, organize events, and provide mentorship opportunities for Black students interested in computer science. Collaboration with NSBC can improve the visibility of computer science programs among Black communities.

Black Boys Code

Black Boys Code is a nonprofit organization that focuses on empowering Black boys and young men with essential coding skills. Schools can collaborate with this organization to host coding workshops, hackathons, and STEM camps targeted specifically at Black male students. By nurturing early interest in computer science, schools can cultivate a pipeline of talented Black students.

Black Code Collective

This community-driven initiative aims to connect Black computer science students and professionals. Educational institutions can encourage their Black students to join the Black Code Collective to gain access to networking opportunities, coding projects, and career development resources. This network can be a source of support and inspiration for Black students pursuing computer science.

Black Founders

Black Founders is an organization that focuses on promoting diversity and inclusion in the tech startup ecosystem. Schools can partner with Black Founders to create entrepreneurship and innovation programs that encourage Black students to explore computer science not just as a field of study but as a pathway to entrepreneurial success. This approach can appeal to students with a passion for both technology and business.

Other Useful Methods

A number of other methods can be used to attract both Black and Hispanic students:

- Diverse faculty and role models: Hire a diverse faculty that includes Black and Hispanic computer science professors and professionals who can serve as role models for students. Representation matters, and seeing individuals who have successfully navigated the field can inspire students to pursue computer science.

- Outreach programs: Create outreach programs that target local communities, particularly in underserved areas. These programs can include coding workshops, information sessions, and scholarship opportunities to make computer science education more accessible.

- Mentorship programs: Establish mentorship programs that connect students with mentors who have experience in the computer science industry. These mentors can provide guidance, support, and valuable insights into the field.

- Scholarships and financial aid: Offer scholarships and financial aid packages specifically designed to attract and retain these students in computer science programs. Financial barriers should not prevent talented individuals from pursuing their dreams in technology.

- Supportive environments: Foster inclusive and supportive learning environments where Black and Hispanic students feel comfortable and encouraged to express their ideas and interests in computer science.

- Collaboration with local organizations: Partner with local community organizations that focus on education and empowerment within these communities.

Introducing Culturally Relevant Resources into a Classroom

Creating a culturally inclusive classroom goes beyond just recognizing and celebrating different cultures. It involves integrating culturally relevant resources and perspectives into the curriculum. With that in mind, let's explore practical strategies that you can use to introduce culturally relevant resources into your classroom.

Visual Representation with Diverse Posters

Adding posters and visual displays that showcase the contributions of Black and Hispanic individuals in computer science will help you to create an inclusive atmosphere that reflects the diversity of the field. These posters can feature notable figures such as Grace Hopper, Mark

Dean, Ada Lovelace, or modern-day trailblazers like Kimberly Bryant and Arlan Hamilton.

Student-Created Displays

Encourage your students to take an active role in shaping the classroom environment. Get them to conduct research on Black and Hispanic figures in computer science and create their own displays or presentations. This not only helps students develop research and presentation skills but also allows them to take ownership of their learning and contribute to the cultural richness of the classroom.

Fostering a Safe Learning Space

Encourage questions and discussions about cultural backgrounds and experiences. Recognize that students may come from diverse educational backgrounds and may not have had equal access to resources. Be patient and supportive when addressing gaps in knowledge and skills, and make sure that no one feels left behind.

Connecting Computer Science to Life Experiences

Make computer science relevant to your students' lives by connecting it to their real-world experiences and interests. For example, discuss how computer science is involved in video game development, social media platforms, the creation of mobile apps, or any other topics that resonate with them. Showcasing the practical applications of computer science can make the subject matter more engaging and relatable, and make it feel less abstract.

Listening to Student Voices

Actively seek your students' input on what topics, figures, or projects they find interesting and culturally significant. By including their voices in the decision-making process, you can tailor the curriculum to meet their needs and interests and make them feel more included.

Diverse Literature and Media

Expand the classroom's resource library to include books, articles, and media that represent a wide range of cultural perspectives. Use readings and assignments that highlight the contributions and challenges faced by Black and Hispanic individuals in computer science. This not only provides diverse perspectives but also encourages critical thinking and empathy.

The most underrepresented group in computer science by far is Native Americans. In the following chapter, we will explore why this is the case, and what we can do about it.

Chapter 5

Recruiting Native Americans to Computer Science Classes

I was the only female in my class. I sat on one side of the room and the guys on the other side of the room. I guess they didn't want to associate with me. But I could hold my own with them and sometimes did better.
–Mary Golda Ross

In this chapter we will explore the barriers Native Americans face in computer science and what can be done about this. You will discover techniques to encourage more Native Americans into the classroom and how to help them thrive in the subject.

The Challenge of Increasing Native American Representation in Computer Science

The underrepresentation of Native Americans in computer science is rooted in historical, cultural, and several other systemic factors. While efforts have been made to promote diversity in technology-related fields, the Native American community continues to face unique challenges that hinder their participation. With that in mind, let's explore why we still aren't seeing more Native Americans in computer science and look at the clash between their traditional culture and the culture of computer science.

Historical Disparities

Centuries of colonization, forced relocations (such as the Trail of Tears), and cultural suppression have left a deep and lasting impact on

Native American communities. These events have disrupted traditional ways of life, eroded cultural practices, and resulted in socioeconomic disparities.

Native American communities have often faced unequal access to educational resources, leading to disparities in academic achievement. In computer science, this historical disadvantage translates into fewer opportunities and fewer Native American students pursuing careers in technology.

Cultural Differences

Native American culture is deeply rooted in holistic and humanistic values. Native Americans have traditionally embraced a communal approach to learning and success, which often contrasts with the individualistic and competitive culture prevalent in computer science and the tech industry at large. In many Native communities, modesty and humility are highly regarded, and boasting about personal achievements is considered taboo.

This cultural difference can create a disconnect between Native American students and the self-promotion often necessary to thrive in tech careers. Native American students may be less inclined to assert themselves in competitive environments, which may lead to missed opportunities.

Educational Barriers

As we said earlier, the most significant barrier for Native American students in computer science education is the lack of access to quality education. Many Native communities struggle with inadequate funding for schools, resulting in overcrowded classrooms, outdated materials, and a shortage of experienced teachers. These factors contribute to a less than optimal learning environment, especially considering how quickly schools can fall behind modern technology, making it challenging for students to develop a strong foundation in computer science.

The absence of advanced STEM courses and resources in many Native American schools limits the opportunities for students to explore and excel in computer science. This lack of exposure to rigorous STEM curriculum places Native American students at a disadvantage when pursuing computer science at higher levels.

Cultural Biases in Educational Materials

Most computer science textbooks and even curricula fail to include perspectives of Native American communities. This omission can make it difficult for Native American students to relate to, as they may not see themselves reflected in the educational materials.

To address these educational barriers, several strategies can be implemented:

- Increase funding: Advocating for increased funding for schools in Native American communities is vital. Adequate resources—such as updated materials, technology, and well-trained teachers—are needed to provide quality education.

- Culturally relevant curriculum: Developing culturally relevant curriculum materials that incorporate Native American history, culture, and contributions can engage and empower Native American students in STEM subjects.

- Teacher training: Provide professional development opportunities for teachers in Native American communities. Focus on STEM education best practices and cultural sensitivity.

Limited Resources

Native American communities often face challenges in providing access to technology for students. Many households lack computers or internet connectivity, making engaging in online learning or accessing computer science resources difficult. This digital divide worsens the educational disparities faced by Native American youth, because even if they are interested in pursuing a career in computer sciences, they lack access to the modern technology and information they need to follow their interests.

Mentorship and Guidance

Many Native American students may have limited access to mentors who can guide them through the complexities of computer science. As we've seen with other groups, a lack of role models and mentors can deter students from pursuing computer science as a career path. There are three main ways to combat this lack of resources, though not all can be done by one person. These are:

- Infrastructure development: Invest in improving technology infrastructure in Native American communities, including expanding internet access and providing devices to students.

- Virtual mentorship programs: Establish virtual mentorship programs that connect Native American students with professionals in the computer science field. These programs can offer guidance, support, and inspiration.

- Community partnerships: Collaborate with local organizations, businesses, and universities to provide Native Americans with resources such as computer labs and access to technology.

Stereotypes and Bias

Stereotypes and biases within the tech industry can perpetuate misconceptions about Native Americans. These misconceptions may include assumptions about skill levels, capabilities, or relevance to the field. These stereotypes can limit Native American individuals' opportunities in tech and hinder their professional growth. These can be combatted in the following ways:

- Representation matters: Promote the inclusion of Native American professionals in tech-related positions and highlight their accomplishments in order to challenge stereotypes and provide positive role models for Native American students.

- Implicit bias training: Offer training to tech industry professionals to raise awareness about unconscious biases and provide strategies for combatting them.

Community Engagement

Collaborating with community leaders and educators can help develop culturally sensitive programs that align with traditional values and beliefs. These programs can make computer science more appealing and relevant to Native American youth.

Creating initiatives that work with, not against, indigenous perspectives and knowledge can be major steppingstone to improving Native American involvement in the field. This not only makes computer science more engaging but also demonstrates the value of Native American contributions to all STEM fields.

Efforts should be made to celebrate Native American cultural within the curriculum. This can involve incorporating cultural elements into curriculum materials and lessons, such as indigenous examples in coding projects or discussions of traditional ecological knowledge in data science.

Showcasing Successful Native American Professionals

Emphasizing the stories of successful Native American professionals can inspire younger generations. These role models demonstrate to Native American students that they can overcome barriers and pursue careers in computer science while staying true to their cultural identity.

Let's take a look at some of these role models who you can use to inspire your students.

Kimberly Clavin

Kimberly Clavin is a proud member of the Choctaw Nation, with deep roots in Native American culture. As the founder of the Native American Program at Google, Clavin has made substantial contributions to advancing diversity and inclusion initiatives in the tech industry. Her role at Google has been important in creating opportunities for Native Americans to thrive in the technology sector. Under her leadership, the Native American Program at Google has launched several initiatives, including scholarships, mentorship programs, and community outreach efforts. These initiatives aim to increase the representation of Native Americans in technology roles, encourage STEM education among Native American youth, and provide resources and support for their professional development.

Dr. John Herrington

Dr. John Herrington is a Chickasaw astronaut and computer scientist with a remarkable background in both space exploration and technology. Herrington made history as the first enrolled member of a Native American tribe to fly in space. He actively engages in STEM outreach, using his experiences to inspire and educate Native American students. Through these efforts, he emphasizes the importance of pursuing education and careers in STEM fields, breaking down barriers and fostering a sense of possibility among Native American youth.

Dr. Jessie Little Doe Baird

Dr. Jessie Little Doe Baird is a member of the Mashpee Wampanoag Tribe. Baird is renowned for her groundbreaking work in language revitalization technology. Through her expertise in linguistics and computer science, she has played an important role in preserving and reviving indigenous languages, particularly the Wampanoag language.

Baird's work involves the development of innovative language-learning software and resources that make use of technology to teach and preserve Native American languages. Her contributions are helping in maintaining cultural identity and heritage within Native American communities. By combining her passion for linguistics with her proficiency in computer science, Dr. Jessie Little Doe Baird has revived languages on the brink of extinction and paved the way for others to use technology as a tool for cultural preservation and revitalization.

Ryan Red Corn

Ryan Red Corn is a member of the Osage Nation. Red Corn is a cofounder of Buffalo Nickel Creative, a multimedia company that blends technology and storytelling to share Native American perspectives with the world. Through innovative multimedia projects such as films, digital content, and interactive experiences, Red Corn's work serves as a platform for Native American voices. His storytelling prowess, combined with technological innovation, has helped to communicate the richness of Native American cultures. He also has demonstrated the potential for Native Americans to contribute significantly to the tech world while preserving their cultural heritage.

These are but a handful of the Native Americans who have found success in the industry. Encourage your students to dig deeper into other Native Americans who have been successful and find role models who speak to them on a personal level.

Networking to Increase Native American Enrollment in Computer Science Education

The tech industry's rapid growth and the increasing importance of digital literacy in the modern world have highlighted the urgency of ensuring that Native American communities have equitable access to computer science education. Several initiatives and events have taken steps to address this issue. These include the Teachers in Native Communities Affinity Group; Indigenous Communities & K-12 CS

Education Virtual Summit; First Steps to Computer Science Education in Our K-12 Schools; and Indigenous Communities & CS Education Panel. Let's explore these initiatives and look at the importance of networking and partnerships in advancing computer science education among Native American communities.

The Naipi Code

The Naipi Code Initiative is designed to champion the cause of computer science education within Native American communities. It recognizes the potential of computer science as a tool for empowerment, and it is firmly rooted in the conviction that a single motivated educator can initiate projects that shape the lives of students. This initiative not only seeks to provide technical knowledge but also to empower Native American youth with skills, opportunities, and a sense of belonging in the digital age.

The initiative focuses on creating a tailored computer science curriculum that respects and incorporates Native American culture and values. The curriculum includes coding, computer programming, software development, and computer literacy, ensuring students are well-equipped for future careers in technology.

Recognizing the importance of educators as catalysts for change, the Naipi Code Initiative offers training programs for teachers within Native American communities. These programs equip them with the skills and knowledge needed to teach computer science in a way tailored to Native American youth. Ongoing professional development and support are provided to ensure educators remain up to date with the latest advancements in technology and pedagogy.

The initiative actively seeks partnerships with tech companies, educational institutions, and philanthropic organizations to secure funding and resources. This ensures that schools in Native American communities have access to state-of-the-art computer labs, software, and textbooks.

Scholarships and grants are also made available to students interested in pursuing higher education in computer science or related fields.

The Teachers in Native Communities Affinity Group

This affinity group serves as a dynamic platform for educators to come together, collaborate, exchange best practices, and craft resources that are not only academic but also culturally resonant and captivating for Native American students. By participating in this network, teachers can tap into a wealth of insights and peer support, enabling them to better serve their students and inspire the next generation of Native American tech leaders.

The affinity group facilitates the collaborative development of culturally relevant computer science resources, lesson plans, and teaching materials. These resources draw from Native American culture, history, and traditions to engage students and make learning meaningful. Educators share their successful teaching strategies, fostering a rich ecosystem of resources that can be adapted to different Native American communities. Regular meetings, both in person and virtually, enable educators to stay connected, learn from one another, and stay updated on the latest developments in computer science education.

To ensure that computer science education is culturally sensitive and inclusive, the affinity group offers training and workshops for educators. These sessions help teachers understand the diverse backgrounds and needs of their students.

The affinity group also takes an active role in advocating for increased funding and resources for computer science education in Native American communities. It engages with policymakers, organizations, and stakeholders to further this cause.

The Indigenous Communities & K-12 CS Education Virtual Summit

The Indigenous Communities & K-12 CS Education Virtual Summit assembles a diverse range of experts, educators, and community leaders with a common mission to address the unique challenges and opportunities in expanding computer science education within Native

American communities. This summit serves as a platform for discussions, knowledge sharing, and collaborative problem-solving, offering a space where stakeholders can come together to create innovative solutions for enhancing Native American enrollment.

The summit features expert panel discussions that dive into the unique challenges and opportunities of computer science education in Native American communities. Panelists, including educators, researchers, policymakers, and industry leaders, share their insights and best practices. Topics include curriculum development, teacher training, funding strategies, cultural relevance, and advocacy efforts tailored to the needs of Native American students.

Practical workshops equip educators with tools, strategies, and resources for delivering effective computer science education in Native American K-12 schools. These workshops focus on developing culturally sensitive curriculum, creating inclusive classrooms, and leveraging technology to improve learning experiences.

The summit provides ample networking opportunities for attendees to connect with like-minded individuals, share their experiences, and forge partnerships. Educators can collaborate with experts, community leaders, and fellow educators, creating a network of support that extends beyond the summit.

First Steps to Computer Science Education in Our K-12 Schools Initiative

This initiative acknowledges the importance of introducing computer science at an early age. It is focused on creating age-appropriate curriculum materials specifically tailored to engage and educate Native American students about the world of computer science. By targeting the early stages of education, this initiative seeks to establish a strong foundation for a lifelong interest in technology and computer science among Native American youth.

First Steps is dedicated to crafting curriculum materials that are age-appropriate, culturally relevant, and engaging for Native American students from kindergarten through 12th grade. Curriculum materials are designed to introduce fundamental computer science concepts in a way that aligns with the developmental stages of students, fostering interest and curiosity.

The initiative actively engages with Native American communities, parents, and guardians to raise awareness about the importance of early computer science education. Workshops, seminars, and outreach programs are organized to involve families in their children's educational journeys and create a supportive learning environment. To ensure that curriculum materials are robust and up to date, the initiative collaborates with educational organizations, experts, and technology companies. Resources, lesson plans, and teaching materials are shared among educators, creating a supportive network for enhancing computer science education.

The Indigenous Communities & CS Education Panel

The Indigenous Communities & CS Education Panel is a platform for experts, advocates, educators, and community leaders to engage in conversations regarding computer science education within Native American communities. This panel discussion is dedicated to addressing the distinct challenges and opportunities that arise in the context of computer science education, offering a space where participants can share insights and learn from one another's experiences.

The panel features experts from various backgrounds, including computer science educators, researchers, policymakers, and advocates. These experts offer valuable insights into the challenges and opportunities of computer science education within Native American communities. Their experiences and research findings help to shape the discourse and provide a deeper understanding of the complexities involved.

Panelists discuss best practices and successful initiatives that have made a positive impact on computer science education in indigenous communities. These practices cover curriculum development, teacher training, cultural relevance, community engagement, and more, offering practical insights for attendees. The panel promotes open and honest dialogue, encouraging participants to ask questions, share their experiences, and seek guidance.

The Role of Partnerships

Partnerships within Native American communities bring together community leaders, teachers, students, and organizations like Naipi Code to collaboratively address the challenges faced by Native American youth and create solutions. By working together, these stakeholders can ensure that computer science education is culturally relevant, accessible, and appealing to Native American students, thereby increasing their contribution to the field.

To create an inclusive classroom, educators must use appropriate terminology, incorporate Native American perspectives into the curriculum, and provide resources to deepen their understanding. With that in mind, let's explore strategies for making Native American students feel like an integral part of their classrooms.

Using Appropriate Terminology

One of the best ways to make Native Americans feel valued in the classroom is using accurate and respectful terminology. Native Circle, an organization dedicated to Native American culture and education, provides a reference list of terms that should be avoided because of their historical and cultural insensitivity. You can refer to this resource to ensure that you are using respectful language when discussing Native American history, culture, and experiences. Doing so will help you create a safe and inclusive space where students can engage with the content without feeling marginalized or disrespected.

State-Provided Native American Lesson Plans

Most states offer Native American lesson plans that align with curriculum standards. These lesson plans not only provide educators with guidance on incorporating Native American history, culture, and contributions into their teaching, but also ensure that the content is accurate, culturally sensitive, and respectful. You can use these resources to improve your lessons and create a more inclusive educational experience for all students.

Real-World Examples of Native American Innovations

Incorporating real-world examples of Native American innovations into the curriculum is another great way to make Native American students feel valued in the classroom. Native Americans have a rich history of scientific and technological advancements, from agricultural innovations to medicinal knowledge, but your students may not be aware of this. You can highlight these contributions by adding them into lessons, showing students that Native Americans have made significant and ongoing contributions to society. This not only promotes a sense of pride and recognition among your Native American students, but also educates all students about the diversity and richness of Native American cultures.

Additional Resources for Teachers

To assist you in your efforts to create an inclusive classroom environment, you'll need comprehensive resources. You can benefit from educational organizations and websites that offer a wealth of information and materials related to Native American culture and education. Let's look at some of these resources below:

- Native Circle: Native Circle's website offers a range of educational materials, lesson plans, and resources that promote cultural understanding and sensitivity.

- National Indian Education Association: NIEA is an organization dedicated to advancing Native education. Their website provides resources, policy updates, and best practices for educators.

- Tribal Nations Maps: Providing maps and information about specific tribal nations can help students better understand the diversity of Native American cultures.

- Smithsonian National Museum of the American Indian: The museum's website offers educational materials, videos, and lesson plans that can be integrated into the curriculum.

Computer science, especially when it comes to coding, has its own language. Students whose first language isn't English need additional support in navigating the computer science classroom. In the next chapter we will go through the challenges faced by students whose first language isn't English, and the steps you can take to improve their understand of the subject.

Chapter 6

Empowering English Language Learners in Computer Science Education

Learning another language is not only learning different words for the same things, but learning another way to think about things.
–Flora Lewis

The barriers English language learners (ELL) students face are fairly self-explanatory, so while we will touch on them in this chapter, we will be more focused on the strategies you can employ to help non-native speakers, as well as methods for developing an inclusive learning environment.

How English Language Learners Get Left Behind

English has emerged as the global lingua franca, transcending borders and cultures to become the predominant language of science, technology, commerce, and academia. Its influence extends to almost every aspect of our modern lives, from the Internet to textbooks, from research to international collaborations. You'll be hard pressed to find a corner of the world where the people don't know at least some English, if even just a word or two. However, amid this dominance of English, the plight of English language learners who struggle to keep pace with the linguistic demands of an increasingly interconnected world often goes unnoticed. ELLs often get left behind in their pursuit of knowledge and career opportunities, especially within computer science.

The English Barrier in Education

English proficiency is essential for academic success, especially in fields like computer science and engineering. ELLs, while possessing strong skills in their respective fields, often find themselves at a disadvantage due to language barriers. They need to take language-intensive entrance exams and interviews, where they must compete against native English speakers, setting the tone for future challenges.

Lack of Access to Resources

Many ELLs come from regions where English is not the first language, and they might not have access to the same quality of English language education and resources as their English-speaking counterparts. This lack of access to resources can hinder their ability to develop fluency in English.

Linguistic Bias in Academia

ELLs may struggle to comprehend complex research papers, textbooks, or lectures, making it difficult for them to keep up with their coursework and expand their knowledge base, especially when there are few, if any, translations available. This bias can inadvertently exclude talented individuals from pursuing academic or research careers.

Group Work and Collaboration

Working in groups where English is the common language often can be difficult. Miscommunication and misunderstandings can impede progress and hinder the contributions of ELLs, leading to isolation and frustration.

Unequal Opportunities

English proficiency is often a prerequisite for scholarships, research grants, and internships in English-speaking countries. This requirement can exclude talented ELLs from accessing these opportunities, limiting their academic and professional growth.

Thesis and Publications

In computer science and engineering, students are expected to produce theses and research papers in English. Many other STEM fields also have this requirement. ELLs face an uphill battle in meeting these expectations because they must not only conduct groundbreaking research but also present it in a new language.

Career Limitations

Even beyond academia, proficiency in English is increasingly vital for career advancement. In computer science and engineering, professionals often collaborate with colleagues from around the world, present their work at international conferences, and publish in English-language journals. ELLs may find their career prospects limited and their contributions undervalued.

Tatsuya Amano's Experiences

To shed light on the challenges faced by ELLs in fields like computer science and engineering, it may be useful to look at a real world example, Tatsuya Amano.

Tatsuya Amano is a highly talented computer scientist from Japan, a country known for its technological innovations. He excelled in his early education and was passionate about pursuing a career in computer science. However, his journey took a unique turn when he decided to pursue further studies and a career in an English-speaking country.

Amano's first major challenge came during the application process for international universities. English proficiency tests like the TOEFL and IELTS were prerequisites for admission. Although he was a brilliant computer scientist, he struggled with the language components of these exams. He dedicated months to language preparation, and despite his best efforts, he faced a linguistic barrier.

Upon joining a prestigious university in the United States, Amano discovered that a significant portion of the coursework, research papers, and textbooks were in English. While he had a solid grasp of computer science concepts, comprehending advanced topics presented in English proved to be a formidable challenge. He often spent extra hours translating materials into his native Japanese to fully understand them.

Participation in group projects and research collaborations exposed Amano to another set of challenges. Although he could communicate effectively in basic conversations, participating in academic discussions and debates required a level of fluency that he had not achieved. This sometimes led to feelings of isolation and frustration as he struggled to contribute meaningfully to collaborative efforts.

The climax of Amano's academic journey was the preparation of his thesis and research publications. While he had made significant contributions to his field, the process of writing and presenting his work in English was grueling. He sought help from language tutors and academic writing centers, but the linguistic barrier remained a significant obstacle. This challenge extended to presenting his research at international conferences, where he had to prepare and practice his presentations to compensate for language limitations.

Upon completing his studies, Amano entered the job market with a solid academic record but continued to face career limitations due to his English proficiency. While he was an exceptional computer scientist, his non-native English-speaking background often led to overlooked opportunities. Many employers sought individuals with stronger language skills.

Amano's experiences exemplify the hurdles that many English language learners face when pursuing careers in fields dominated by the English language. Despite his exceptional talent and determination, linguistic barriers posed substantial challenges throughout his academic life and professional career (Lenharo, 2023).

Amano's story shows the importance of recognizing and addressing the needs of ELLs in these fields. Institutions and educators should provide additional support, language resources, and mentorship opportunities to help ELLs bridge the linguistic gap. By doing so, we can ensure that talented individuals like Amano are not left behind, which doesn't just harm them, but the field as a whole.

Resources for Your ELL Students

Fortunately, several valuable resources available online can help your ELL students improve their English language skills while gaining proficiency in computer science and IT concepts. Below are several websites they can use, and what these sites provide.

Lingua House

(https://www.linguahouse.com/esl-lesson-plans/vocabulary/computing)

Resource type: ESL lesson plans

Lingua House offers a collection of ESL lesson plans tailored to the vocabulary related to computing. These lesson plans include detailed instructions for teachers and a variety of activities that help ELLs build their computer-related English language skills.

iSLCollective

(https://en.islcollective.com/english-esl-worksheets/search/computer)

Resource type: ESL worksheets

iSLCollective provides a vast repository of ESL worksheets focused on computer-related topics. Teachers and students can access and download worksheets that cover computer terminology, basic concepts, and more.

ESL Brains

Resource type: ESL lesson plans

ESL Brains offers lesson plans related to technology, making it a valuable resource for ELLs interested in computer science. These lesson plans incorporate real-world scenarios and are designed to engage students in discussions and activities centered around technology and IT.

Your English Pal

Resource type: ESL conversation lesson plans

Your English Pal provides ESL conversation lesson plans with a focus on computers. These lesson plans are designed to improve students' English conversation skills while exploring various computer-related topics.

British Council Learn English Kids

Resource type: Educational materials for kids

British Council's LearnEnglish Kids platform offers a range of resources geared toward young ELLs interested in computers and technology. These materials include interactive games, videos, and worksheets, making learning engaging for children.

Fluentbe

Resource type: English for IT resources

Fluentbe provides a curated list of English resources specifically tailored for IT and computer science learners. These resources cover various IT-related topics, including coding, software development, and IT project management.

Brilliant

Resource type: Online courses

Brilliant offers online courses that teach computer science basics. While it's a paid platform, it provides comprehensive and interactive lessons suitable for both beginners and intermediate learners. ELLs can improve their computer science knowledge while improving their English language skills. As a bonus, they offer special rates for educators looking to use the platform to teach their students, truly... brilliant!

Breaking Language Barriers in Computer Science

Several notable computer scientists have successfully broken language barriers, achieving global recognition despite English not being their first language, and they may be an inspiration to your ELL students who doubt their abilities. Let's look at the stories of four such pioneers who have made significant contributions to the world of computing.

Sergey Brin

Sergey Brin, born in Moscow, Russia, in 1973, is one of the co-founders of Google, one of the most influential tech companies in the world. He moved to the United States with his family at the age of 6. While his family spoke Russian at home, Sergey quickly adapted to English. He later attended Stanford University, where he met Larry Page, with whom he later co-founded Google.

Sergey Brin's contributions to the development of the Google search engine and the subsequent growth of Google as a tech giant are widely celebrated. His success demonstrates the ability to excel in the English-dominated tech world, even as a non-native English speaker.

Satoshi Nakamoto

Satoshi Nakamoto is the pseudonymous creator of Bitcoin, the world's first cryptocurrency, and the underlying blockchain technology. While

Nakamoto's true identity remains a mystery, the Bitcoin white paper and early communications associated with the cryptocurrency suggest Japanese origins.

Nakamoto's groundbreaking creation, Bitcoin, has revolutionized finance and technology. The use of a pseudonym allowed Nakamoto to break language barriers and make a global impact, transcending linguistic and cultural boundaries.

Guido Van Rossum

Guido Van Rossum, a Dutch programmer, created the Python programming language in the late 1980s while working at the Centrum Wiskunde & Informatica (CWI) in the Netherlands. He initially developed Python as a side project but later released it to the world.

Python has become one of the world's most popular programming languages, known for its simplicity and readability. Van Rossum's ability to create a programming language that transcends linguistic boundaries has had a profound impact on the global tech community.

Edsger W. Dijkstra

Edsger W. Dijkstra was a Dutch computer scientist who made significant contributions to computer science, particularly in the areas of algorithms and software engineering. He conducted most of his groundbreaking research and work while based in the Netherlands.

Dijkstra's work on algorithms and programming languages laid the foundation for modern computer science. Despite primarily working in Dutch academia, his contributions are celebrated worldwide, showing the universality of his ideas.

Teaching Strategies to Boost Communication

In the context of computer science, or any technical field, having clear and open communication between educators and students is essential for understanding complex concepts, solving problems, and creating a positive learning environment. Let's explore several teaching strategies that you can adapt for your CS classroom. As a bonus, these strategies not only help ELL students, but native speakers, too!

- Active listening: Active listening involves giving students your full attention, asking clarifying questions, and showing empathy. In CS, where abstract concepts can be challenging, active listening helps identify students' specific difficulties and allows you to tailor explanations and support accordingly.

- Clear and structured communication: Present information clearly and in a structured manner. This includes providing clear instructions, organizing lectures logically, and using visual aids, diagrams, and coding examples to illustrate concepts effectively.

- Encourage questions and discussion: Create an open and inclusive classroom atmosphere where students feel comfortable asking questions and engaging in discussions. Encouraging questions improves critical thinking and ensures that students understand the material.

- Feedback loop: Establish a feedback loop that allows students to provide feedback on the course, teaching methods, and materials. Regularly seek input and use it to adapt your teaching approach to meet students' needs.

- Adapt to diverse learning styles: Recognize that students have different learning styles. Some may excel in hands-on coding, while others may prefer visual or auditory learning. Offer a variety of learning resources and activities to accommodate these differences.

- Use technology wisely: Leverage technology, such as online forums, video lectures, and collaborative coding platforms, to improve communication and facilitate discussion both inside and outside the classroom. These tools can promote engagement and collaboration among students.

- Real-world relevance: Connect CS concepts to real-world applications and case studies. Show how what they are learning is relevant in the tech industry or other fields. This can inspire motivation and engagement.

- Break down complex concepts: When teaching complex CS topics, break them down into smaller, more digestible pieces. Encourage students to tackle problems step by step, providing guidance and feedback at each stage.

- Active learning and group work: Incorporate active learning strategies, such as group projects and problem-solving exercises. Group work not only encourages collaboration but also enhances communication skills as students discuss and share ideas.

- Office hours and one-on-one support: Offer regular office hours and one-on-one support sessions to address individual student concerns or provide additional clarification. This personal attention can be invaluable, especially for students struggling with specific topics.

- Cultivate a growth mindset: Promote a growth mindset by emphasizing that mistakes and challenges are opportunities for growth. Encourage students to persevere through difficulties and see them as part of the learning process.

- Assessment and evaluation: Regularly assess student understanding through quizzes, assignments, and exams. Use these assessments not only to evaluate their knowledge but also as opportunities to provide feedback and identify areas for improvement.

After all these chapters, you possibly are rather overwhelmed. In the next chapter, we will tie all the theories together with tips on how to create an inclusive curriculum.

Chapter 7:

Creating an Inclusive Computer Science Curriculum

Children are better able to learn when the classroom climate is positive, warm, and inviting. Part of being welcomed is seeing your own language and culture reflected throughout all aspects of the classroom.
—Brookes

The aim of this chapter is to provide examples of curricula that welcome and support underrepresented groups in the computer science classroom, along with tips and resources that you can use for your own curriculum.

The Importance of Diverse Curricula in Education

Schools are commonly seen as the foundations of society, where young minds are developed and molded. Within this framework, the curriculum is the fundamental building block of education. Thus, diverse curriculum is significant for several reasons. Let's explore the impact it can have.

Breaking Down Stereotypes

A diverse curriculum can challenge and break down stereotypes that persist in society. Through a diverse range of materials, students are exposed to different cultures, perspectives, and experiences. This exposure encourages critical thinking and helps students to question their preconceived notions. When students learn about the achievements, contributions, and struggles of individuals from diverse backgrounds, it dismantles stereotypes and prejudices that may have been ingrained in their sub-conscious.

Fostering Cultural Sensitivity

Diversity in the curriculum fosters cultural sensitivity and empathy. It enables students to appreciate and respect the rich history of cultures that make up our global community. Exposure to different cultures, histories, and traditions helps students understand the significance of cultural diversity, and this understanding is important for promoting agreement and inclusivity in our increasingly multicultural societies.

Preparing for a Globalized World

Borders are becoming less relevant, and cultures are constantly intermingling, so preparing students for a globalized world is essential. A diverse curriculum equips students with the knowledge and skills they need to engage with people from different backgrounds and navigate the complexities of a global society. It promotes cultural literacy, communication, and a sense of interconnectedness that is invaluable in today's interconnected world.

Encouraging Inclusivity

A diverse curriculum sends a clear message that all voices and perspectives are valued. It ensures that the experiences and contributions of historically marginalized groups are acknowledged and integrated into the educational experience. This inclusivity is not only needed for creating a fair and just society but also for empowering individuals to embrace their own identities and feel a sense of belonging in the classroom and beyond.

Enhancing Critical Thinking and Problem-Solving

Diversity in the curriculum stimulates critical thinking and problem-solving skills. When students encounter a variety of viewpoints and challenges, they are encouraged to think critically, analyze information, and develop well-rounded perspectives. This skill set is not only useful for academic success but also for making informed decisions and contributing to society as engaged and responsible citizens.

Preparing for a Diverse Workforce

As the workforce becomes increasingly diverse, a curriculum that reflects this diversity will aid in preparing students for their future careers. Exposure to diverse perspectives and experiences in the classroom prepares students to work in diverse teams and adapt to different cultural contexts. It also increases their ability to understand and cater to the needs of a diverse customer base.

Considerations for Your Inclusive Curriculum

So how do you go about creating an inclusive curriculum? Let's explore three considerations for an inclusive curriculum: learning space, instruction, and curricular materials.

Learning Space

The physical and emotional aspects of the learning environment play an important role in creating an inclusive curriculum. These include:

Classroom Arrangement

Consider the physical arrangement of the classroom. Make sure that it is flexible and adaptable to accommodate diverse learning needs. Arrange seating in a way that promotes interaction and inclusivity.

Providing options for various seating arrangements, such as group tables, individual desks, and comfortable seating, can cater to different learning preferences and needs.

Accessibility

An inclusive classroom must be accessible to all students. This includes providing ramps, elevators, and designated spaces for students with physical disabilities. You may also want to consider the needs of students with sensory sensitivities, such as creating quiet areas and providing noise-canceling headphones for those who require them.

Emotional Safety

An inclusive learning space should be emotionally safe for all students. Teachers must establish clear expectations for respectful behavior and address issues like bullying or discrimination promptly. Encourage open dialogue among students to create a supportive atmosphere where differences are respected and celebrated.

Instruction

Effective instruction is at the heart of an inclusive curriculum. To make sure that every student has access to high-quality learning experiences, you'll need to think about three main things:

Differentiation

You should employ differentiation strategies to cater to diverse learning styles and abilities within the classroom. This might involve providing alternative assignments, using multimedia resources, or offering additional support for struggling students. Tailoring instruction to individual needs empowers every student to succeed.

Universal Design for Learning (UDL)

Implement UDL principles in lesson planning. This approach involves providing multiple means of representation, engagement, and expression. By incorporating varied teaching methods, materials, and assessments, you can better meet the diverse needs of your students.

Culturally Responsive Teaching

Culturally responsive teaching acknowledges the cultural backgrounds and experiences of students. Using culturally relevant materials and teaching approaches helps students connect with the curriculum, feel valued, and see themselves represented in their education.

Curricular Materials

The last, but in no way least, factor is the choice of curricular materials. These decisions are an important aspect of creating an inclusive curriculum, and should include the following considerations:

Diverse Literature and Resources

Make sure that curricular materials represent a wide range of perspectives, cultures, and backgrounds. Diverse literature, historical accounts, and resources help students gain a more comprehensive understanding of the world and the people who inhabit it.

Accessibility of Materials

Make sure that all curricular materials are accessible to students with disabilities. This may involve providing digital formats, large print options, or audio resources. Additionally, consider offering materials in multiple languages to support English language learners.

Ongoing Evaluation

Regularly assess and update curricular materials to reflect the evolving needs and demographics of your student body. Stay informed about emerging educational resources and trends to ensure that your curriculum remains inclusive and relevant.

Resources for Building an Inclusive Curriculum

An inclusive curriculum recognizes the diversity of learners and aims to ensure equitable access to knowledge and opportunities for all. Let's explore how to choose resources that include the underrepresented, focusing on open-ended activities, accessibility, and promoting collaboration.

Prioritize Open-Ended Activities

Use open-ended activities as a means for students to share their life experiences and problem-solving skills. Open-ended tasks empower students to draw from their unique perspectives, encouraging inclusivity by valuing diverse approaches to problem-solving.

Allow students to celebrate their mistakes during tasks. Encourage reflection on what they've learned, emphasizing the importance of resilience and learning from failures. Incorporate debugging or problem-solving sessions within lessons or topics to create a safe space for such discussions.

Explore opportunities for participatory data collection, where students gather data so they can understand the challenges, decisions, and uses of the data. Hands-on, experiential learning allows everyone to participate and promotes inclusivity.

Ensure Accessibility

Prioritize accessibility when selecting curricular materials. Ensure that language is simple and easy to understand for students who speak English as an additional language. Consider translating instructions or media into multiple languages or incorporating key symbols representing specific activities. Verify that abbreviations, jargon, or technical terms are universally understood.

Evaluate images and videos for accessibility, including the availability of captions and transcripts that can be translated into multiple languages. Be aware of potential cultural interpretations of images and symbols.

Promote Collaboration and Structured Group Discussion

Encourage structured group discussions that reflect industry practices, such as pair programming and team projects. These collaborative approaches mirror real-world scenarios and prepare students for diverse workplace environments.

Address computing-related issues concerning ethics, equity, diversity, inclusion, and social justice within the curriculum. Ensure that structured discussion formats are culturally inclusive, allowing multiple perspectives to be heard and respected. Use structured discussions for formative assessment to gauge student understanding of concepts and identify misconceptions, promoting an inclusive learning environment that values individual progress.

Incorporate Diverse Examples

When selecting learning materials, consider whether they draw on a range of cultural contexts. Diverse examples ensure that students from various backgrounds can relate to and engage with the content. Make sure that learning materials provide multiple perspectives on social, political, and ethical issues, including those relevant to different cultural groups. This encourages critical thinking and a more comprehensive understanding of complex topics.

Exploring Example Curriculums

While some educational institutions guard their curricula closely, resources are available that can serve as exemplars of inclusive curriculum design. Following are several example curricula from government sources, nonprofit organizations, and corporations. We can examine how they contribute to the goal of creating more inclusive educational experiences.

Government Sources: National Curriculum in England (Computing Programs of Study)

Government curriculum guidelines such as those provided by the National Curriculum in England often emphasize a structured approach to education, detailing learning objectives and standards for various key stages. These guidelines ensure that every student, regardless of their background or location, has access to a standardized, high-quality education. They set the stage for a common understanding of what should be included in a computing curriculum, promoting equity in education.

Nonprofit Organizations: Exploring Computer Science Curriculum

Nonprofit organizations like Exploring Computer Science offer curriculum resources that are specifically designed to be inclusive. Their curriculum emphasizes equity, diversity, and inclusion in computer science education.

This curriculum model is centered around the idea that computer science should be accessible to all students, regardless of their prior experience or background. It incorporates topics that resonate with students from diverse communities and fosters an inclusive classroom environment.

Industry Collaboration: Amazon and Code.org Curriculum

Collaborations between corporations like Amazon and nonprofit organizations like Code.org can result in curriculum resources that aim to bridge the gap in computer science education. They often focus on diversity and inclusion initiatives.

These types of partnerships are instrumental in creating curriculum resources that reflect the real-world needs of the technology industry. They emphasize the importance of diversity in tech and prepare students from all backgrounds for careers in the field.

University-Level Curriculum: Canon Lab's Scratch Encore Modules

University-based resources like Canon Lab's Scratch Encore Modules often provide advanced materials designed to deepen students' understanding of computer science concepts. These modules offer an opportunity for students to explore computer science in greater depth and engage with advanced topics. While not designed exclusively for K-12 education, they can support diverse learners who are seeking a more comprehensive understanding of computing.

State-Level Standards: New York State Computer Science and Digital Fluency Learning Standards

State-level standards like those in New York provide a framework for computer science education that aligns with broader educational goals and standards. These standards ensure that computer science is integrated into the broader curriculum, emphasizing its importance alongside other subjects. This approach can help make sure that all students have access to computer science education.

Nonprofit Innovation: ProjectSTEM

Collaborations between ProjectSTEM, a nonprofit innovator, and various stakeholders are reshaping STEM education. They prioritize diversity and inclusion, producing curriculum resources that align with tech industry demands and prepare students for diverse careers in the field. By partnering with industry leaders, ProjectSTEM aims to provide students with the knowledge and skills that are in high demand in the job market, and ultimately prepare them for successful and fulfilling careers.

An inclusive curriculum with be far more effective when there is a community of people ready to offer mentorship, guidance, and positive role models to students from all backgrounds. We will discover how you can do this in the next chapter.

Chapter 8:

Building a Supportive Community and Partnerships

When schools, families, and community groups work together to support learning, children tend to do better in school, stay in school longer, and like school more!
–Anne Henderson and Karen Mapp

In this chapter we will explore how you can reach out to experts near and far to create a network of support for your students, whether through local organizations or larger communities within the computer science field.

How Community Involvement Can Help Address Underrepresentation in Computer Science Education

Community involvement in schools has the potential to create a ripple effect, benefiting teachers, students, and the institutions themselves. Community engagement contributes to fixing underrepresentation in computer science in many ways.

Fostering Accountability and Transparency

Community involvement in schools promotes accountability and transparency within the educational system. When parents, local businesses, and community members actively participate in school activities, they become more invested in the quality of education provided. This increased scrutiny encourages educators to maintain high standards and be more accountable for their teaching methods and outcomes.

Accountability extends to curriculum choice, too, ensuring that computer science education is not only available but also aligned with industry standards and inclusive of diverse perspectives. Community members can participate in curriculum development committees, ensuring that computer science programs are designed to be accessible to a wide range of students, regardless of their backgrounds.

Improving Attendance and Behavior

Community involvement in schools has been shown to have a positive impact on student attendance and behavior. When students feel a strong sense of belonging and support from their community, they are more likely to attend school regularly and exhibit better behavior. This is particularly useful in addressing underrepresentation in computer science, as consistent attendance is needed for mastering complex technical skills.

Community programs can provide incentives for students to attend school regularly, such as scholarships, mentorship opportunities, or extracurricular activities related to computer science. These initiatives not only boost attendance but also create a positive learning environment that encourages students to excel.

Enhancing Student Achievement

Greater community involvement tends to correlate with improved student achievement. When students receive support from their community, they are more likely to set higher goals and work diligently to achieve them. This is especially important where students face steep learning curves and challenges.

Community members can provide mentorship, tutoring, or career guidance, helping students navigate the intricacies of computer science. Local businesses and tech professionals can offer internships, workshops, or guest lectures, exposing students to real-world applications of computer science concepts and motivating them to excel.

Boosting School Reputation

Schools that actively engage their communities tend to enjoy enhanced reputations. This is particularly beneficial when addressing underrepresentation in computer science, as a positive reputation can attract a more diverse student body. When schools are perceived as inclusive and supportive of students from all backgrounds, they become more appealing to a wider range of learners.

Community involvement can also lead to increased funding opportunities and partnerships with local organizations. These collaborations can provide schools with additional resources for improving computer science education, such as updated equipment, specialized training for teachers, or scholarships for underrepresented students.

Strategies for Building Effective Community Partnerships in Education

Partnerships between local businesses and schools can significantly impact the quality of education and contribute to addressing underrepresentation in computer science. Two main types of programs that facilitate such partnerships are school-to-career activities (career awareness programs) and corporate sponsorship programs (adopt-a-school programs). Let's explore these two types of partnerships and provide practical guidelines you can apply for successful collaborations.

School-to-Career Activities (Career Awareness Programs)

School-to-career activities, also known as career awareness programs, play an important role in exposing students to various career paths in the fields of computer science. These programs are designed to bridge the gap between classroom learning and real-world applications. They can take the form of workshops, seminars, or mentorship programs. When planning these activities, consider the following:

- Alignment with curriculum: Ensure that the activities offered through these partnerships align with the school curriculum. This could involve organizing coding workshops, tech career panels, or visits to local tech companies.

- Diverse representation: Encourage local businesses to provide a diverse group of role models and mentors, showing that computer science is an inclusive field open to individuals of all backgrounds.

- Hands-on learning: Emphasize hands-on learning experiences that allow students to apply what they've learned in the classroom to real-world scenarios. For example, students can work on projects with local businesses, gaining practical skills and exposure.

- Assessment and feedback: Establish a feedback loop to assess the effectiveness of these activities. Gather input from both students and teachers to continually improve the partnership's impact on career awareness and education.

Corporate Sponsorship Programs (Adopt-a-School Programs)

Corporate sponsorship programs, often referred to as adopt-a-school programs, involve businesses or organizations partnering with specific schools to provide financial support, resources, and expertise. These partnerships can have a massive impact on the quality of education, especially in areas where resources are limited. When looking join or set up such a program, consider the following:

- Clear goals and expectations: Define clear goals and expectations for the partnership, ensuring that both parties understand their roles and responsibilities. This may include financial support, resource allocation, or mentorship opportunities.

- Long-term commitment: Encourage businesses to commit to long-term partnerships with schools. This stability allows for sustained support and the development of trust between the two entities.

- Tailored support: Customize the support provided to meet the specific needs of the school. This could involve funding for technology upgrades, teacher training, or scholarships for underrepresented students.

- Regular communication: Establish regular communication channels between the school and the sponsoring business. This helps in monitoring progress, addressing challenges, and celebrating successes.

Leveraging Parental Involvement for Enhanced Classroom Success

The active participation of parents in school activities is a valuable asset that can lead to improved student attendance, behavior, and grades, and the development of good social skills. It also plays a role in instilling a lifelong love of learning. Recognizing that not all parents are equally tech-savvy, let's look at some practical ideas to encourage and optimize parental involvement in the classroom while emphasizing inclusivity and diversity.

- Open house and orientation events: Host regular open house events where parents can meet teachers and administrators, learn about the curriculum, and understand school goals.

- Parent-teacher conferences: Schedule regular conferences to discuss student progress, allowing parents to actively engage in their child's education.

- Family workshops: Organize workshops on various topics—including technology literacy, study strategies, and parenting skills—to empower parents in supporting their children's learning.

- Volunteer opportunities: Offer opportunities for parents to volunteer in classrooms, libraries, or school events, accommodating various skill levels and time commitments.

- Parent advisory committees: Establish parent advisory committees that provide input on school policies, programs, and initiatives, ensuring diverse perspectives are considered.

- Family reading programs: Encourage parents to participate in family reading programs, promoting literacy and fostering a love for learning, irrespective of technological prowess.

- Multilingual resources: Provide multilingual resources and communication channels to accommodate parents who speak languages other than English.

- Parent-teacher associations: Promote active involvement in PTAs, where parents can participate in fundraising, event planning, and school improvement projects.

- Digital literacy classes: Offer beginner-level digital literacy classes to help parents navigate technology effectively, enabling them to support their child's online learning.

- Parenting workshops: Organize workshops focusing on parenting skills, including communication, motivation, and addressing academic challenges, irrespective of technological expertise.

- Cultural and diversity celebrations: Host events celebrating the diverse cultural backgrounds of students and their families, fostering a sense of community and inclusion.

- Homework help centers: Create homework help centers, either in-person or online, where parents can assist students with assignments and receive guidance if needed.

- Parent-student projects: Encourage joint parent-student projects that don't rely heavily on technology, such as science experiments, art projects, or gardening initiatives.

- Parent resource libraries: Establish resource libraries with books, guides, and educational materials that parents can borrow to support their child's learning journey.

- Recognition and appreciation: Recognize and appreciate parental involvement through certificates, awards, or public acknowledgments to encourage continued participation.

How Partnerships Drive Diversity in Computer Science

The future of diversity in computer science is a collective commitment shared by educators, students, and industry giants. Large corporations such as Google, Microsoft, and Apple have also recognized the transformative power of partnerships with schools and universities. Their initiatives and collaborations benefit students while shedding light on the mission of the programs.

Google's CS First Program

Google's CS First program aims to empower educators to teach computer science to elementary and middle school students. Through this initiative, Google provides free resources, curriculum materials, and training to teachers, making computer science education more accessible. By engaging students at a young age, Google fosters early interest in computer science, contributing to a diverse talent pool for the future. Students gain foundational skills and confidence in their ability to explore the tech industry.

Microsoft's Imagine Academy

Microsoft's Imagine Academy offers a broad array of technology courses to schools and universities worldwide. It provides curriculum support, software resources, and certifications that prepare students for careers in technology. Students who participate in Microsoft's Imagine Academy gain not only technical skills but also industry-recognized certifications. This equips them for well-paying jobs and reduces the gap between academia and the job market.

Apple's Everyone Can Code Program

Apple's Everyone Can Code program is designed to make coding education accessible to all, with a focus on K-12 schools and community colleges. It provides a comprehensive curriculum and tools for teaching coding and app development. Apple's initiative empowers students with coding skills, enhancing their problem-solving abilities and creativity. This inclusivity contributes to a diverse tech ecosystem by removing barriers to entry.

Benefits of These Programs on Students

These programs have several benefits for students, such as:

Enhanced Career Opportunities

The programs offered by tech giants like Google, Microsoft, and Apple significantly enhance career opportunities for students. These initiatives provide students with valuable skills and certifications that are directly applicable to the tech industry. This skill development opens doors to a wide range of job opportunities within the sector.

Students who participate in these programs gain a competitive edge in the job market. Industry-recognized certifications and hands-on experience make them more attractive candidates to potential employers. By equipping students with the skills needed for tech careers, these programs empower them to pursue well-paying jobs, thereby improving their economic prospects and contributing to upward mobility.

Broadened Access

The partnerships forged between tech corporations and educational institutions have the power to break down barriers to computer science education. These partnerships provide schools and educators with essential resources, including curriculum materials, technology tools, and training. This resource allocation ensures that more schools can offer computer science courses.

By training teachers in computer science instruction, these programs ensure that educators are well-prepared to teach technology-related subjects, even in schools with limited resources. The broadened access extends to schools in underserved communities, allowing students who may not have had previous exposure to computer science the opportunity to explore and excel in this field.

Early Exposure

Initiatives like CS First and Everyone Can Code recognize the importance of introducing computer science concepts to students at an early age. Early exposure ignites curiosity and interest in technology fields, encouraging students to explore and pursue tech-related careers from a young age. As students gain familiarity with computer science concepts early on, they build confidence in their abilities, making them more likely to pursue advanced coursework in the subject.

Inclusivity

These programs are actively working to bridge the diversity gap in the tech industry. Tech giants and educational partnerships are dedicated to reaching out to underrepresented groups in tech, including women, minorities, and individuals with disabilities. By providing pathways for underrepresented students to excel in tech, these programs are creating role models who inspire others to follow in their footsteps, ultimately making the industry more diverse.

The focus on inclusivity is not just about numbers; it's about changing the culture of the tech industry to be more welcoming and inclusive of individuals from diverse backgrounds.

P-TECH

P-TECH, or Pathways in Technology Early College High School, is a groundbreaking initiative that has the mission of forging partnerships between educational institutions and industry leaders. P-TECH schools offer students a unique six-year program that combines high school and college coursework, culminating in an associate degree in a tech-related field. Consider how the program may benefit your students.

The Mission of P-TECH

P-TECH's foremost mission is to break down barriers to quality education, making it accessible to every student, regardless of their socioeconomic background, ethnicity, or prior educational experiences. P-TECH is committed to leveling the educational playing field, making sure that no student is left behind due to circumstances beyond their control. It extends a welcoming hand to those who might face systemic barriers to educational opportunities, including minorities. The program strives to minimize financial obstacles by offering students access to college courses at no cost, removing one of the significant hurdles to higher education.

P-TECH recognizes that education extends beyond textbooks and classrooms. It emphasizes a holistic approach to learning that encompasses not only academics but also practical experiences and mentorship from industry professionals. This education model prepares students for the complexities of the real world. P-TECH's holistic approach ensures that students are equipped with not just theoretical knowledge but also the practical skills and soft skills necessary for success in the tech industry and beyond.

Through these mentorship programs, students receive invaluable guidance from professionals in their chosen fields, offering insights, advice, and encouragement that go beyond what traditional education can provide.

At its core, P-TECH is committed to producing a workforce that is ready and well-prepared for high-paying jobs in technology-related fields immediately upon graduation. It recognizes that education should not be an isolated pursuit but a direct pathway to meaningful employment.

P-TECH schools collaborate closely with industry partners to develop curricula that align with the demands of the job market. This ensures that students are job-ready with skills that are directly applicable to the tech sector.

P-TECH understands that diversity is needed not only for social justice but also for innovation and creativity. It actively dismantles the barriers that have limited access to tech careers for historically marginalized groups. By fostering a diverse and inclusive learning environment, P-TECH aims to produce the next generation of tech leaders who will bring unique perspectives and insights to the industry, ultimately shaping a more equitable and innovative future.

The leap from school to a career in computer sciences may seem like a large step for young people. In the following chapter, you will learn how to guide them through these stages to having a successful career in the field of their dreams, regardless of where they come from.

Chapter 9:

Advanced Placement, Scholarships, Internships, and Career Opportunities

Teach children to be independent learners because a spoon-fed education breeds lazy students. –Jeannie Fulbright

Students, particularly those who don't have family members or role models in the tech industry, may not see a path from computer science classes to the thrilling career of their dreams. Advanced Placement courses, scholarships, and internships may seem out of reach. In this chapter, we'll discuss ways to lead students down the most productive path available.

How AP Courses Open Doors to Opportunities

Advanced Placement courses are a great way for talented students to accelerate their academic success and unlock opportunities. These college-level courses, typically taken in the junior or senior year of high school, offer students a chance to not only deepen their knowledge but also pave the way for college credits, internships, and scholarships. Enrolling in AP courses increases opportunities for your students.

Building Critical Hard and Soft Skills Through AP Courses

Advanced Placement courses teach hard and soft skills, and provide a foundation for future academic and professional life. AP courses are renowned for their challenging curricula, and they expose students to advanced subject matter that often mirrors the content taught in introductory college courses. This prompts students to think critically and engage deeply with complex concepts.

AP courses help to develop critical thinking skills by requiring students to analyze information, solve intricate problems, and make connections between different areas of study. This analytical mindset equips students to approach challenges with confidence. The complexity of AP coursework requires advanced problem-solving skills. Students learn to break down complex problems into manageable components, identify relevant information, and devise effective solutions, all invaluable skills for any academic or professional environment.

Managing the demanding workload of AP courses is an essential skill in itself. Students must learn to juggle multiple assignments, projects, and exams while meeting deadlines. Learning to manage time prepares students for the time-sensitive nature of college and career responsibilities.

College-Level Knowledge

AP courses serve as a bridge between high school and college. They expose students to college-level content, teaching methods, and academic expectations. This familiarity with higher education minimizes the academic shock that some college freshmen experience.

AP courses dive deep into subject matter, allowing students to explore topics in greater detail than standard high school courses. This in-depth understanding is valuable when students encounter related subjects in college, where a strong foundational knowledge is essential.

AP courses require students to develop robust study habits. They learn to manage their time effectively, take thorough notes, and use effective study techniques. These skills prove invaluable throughout their college years.

Cultivating Soft Skills

AP courses help students develop their communication skills. Students must express their thoughts clearly, both in writing and verbally, developing the ability to convey complex ideas coherently, which is a skill that will help them in both academia and the workplace. Many AP courses involve collaborative projects or group discussions. These experiences nurture teamwork and collaboration, preparing students for the collaborative nature of college coursework and professional settings. The challenges presented in AP courses encourage students to adapt and evolve their strategies when faced with new situations or setbacks. This adaptability is a useful skill in an ever-changing world and job market.

Scholarships and Internships

One of the biggest advantages of excelling in AP courses, especially for those without access to a lot of funds, is the potential to earn college credits. Many colleges and universities offer credit or advanced placement to students who score well on AP exams. This can translate into substantial cost savings and an accelerated path to graduation. High achievement in AP courses is also a compelling factor in college admissions. Admissions officers recognize the nature of AP curricula and view them favorably when evaluating applicants. Students who perform well in AP courses are often viewed as motivated, academically prepared, and driven individuals, giving them a better chance of getting into the best universities.

Exceptional performance in AP courses can lead to scholarships and financial aid opportunities. Many institutions and organizations offer scholarships specifically for students with a strong AP track record. These scholarships can significantly reduce the financial burden of higher education. The skills and knowledge acquired in AP courses open doors to internships and research opportunities. Employers and research institutions often seek out students with a strong academic background, offering them hands-on experience that can shape their future careers.

Future Careers

The benefits of excelling in Advanced Placement courses extend far beyond the classroom, and even college. It offers students a clear pathway to future careers. AP courses empower students to align their academic pursuits with their dream jobs.

Career Path Alignment

AP courses provide students with a unique opportunity to explore their academic interests in depth. By diving into subjects they are passionate about, students can gain clarity about their potential career paths. This helps them to make good decisions about their future and select academic and professional pursuits that fit their passions and strengths.

Diverse Career Opportunities

The skills and knowledge acquired through AP courses are versatile and applicable across various industries. Graduates with a strong academic foundation are well-prepared for a wide range of careers. Whether in computer science, STEM fields, humanities, arts, or beyond, the problem-solving, critical thinking, and communication skills developed in AP courses are highly transferable. So even if a student doesn't end up in the computer industry, they will still have greater success than if they hadn't taken the AP course.

Leadership and Innovation

AP courses not only improve subject-specific knowledge but also nurture leadership skills. Students are often required to take on leadership roles in group projects or class discussions, developing their ability to communicate, delegate, and inspire. These leadership skills are highly valued by employers and set the stage for future leadership roles. They may even help students create their own industry changing business one day.

Graduates who excel in AP courses are well-positioned to make meaningful contributions to their professions and society as a whole. Their deep understanding of their chosen fields and their ability to tackle complex challenges equips them to lead, innovate, and effect positive change in their respective domains.

What to Expect From AP Courses

Now that you, and hopefully your students, understand that Advanced Placement courses are a significant steppingstone in high school academics—offering students a unique opportunity to engage in college-level coursework and gain valuable skills and knowledge that can pave the way for future success—it's time to look at what your students should expect from these courses. While each AP course has its own curriculum and objectives, we will look at two popular options: AP Computer Science A and AP Computer Science Principles. Understanding the differences between these two courses and what students can anticipate from each will help you to guide their educational choices.

AP Computer Science A

AP Computer Science A is a rigorous course designed to immerse students in the world of traditional computer programming and fundamental computer science concepts. Throughout the course, students learn the intricacies of a programming language, typically Java, which serves as their primary tool for exploring the subject matter. The curriculum places a strong emphasis on mastering the following areas:

- Programming proficiency: Students learn the syntax and semantics of a programming language, enabling them to write, debug, and optimize code effectively.

- Data structures: They explore various data structures like arrays, lists, and trees, understanding how to organize and manipulate data efficiently.

- Algorithms: Students gain insights into algorithm design and analysis, honing their problem-solving skills by crafting efficient algorithms to solve computational challenges.

- Object-oriented programming: The course covers the principles of object-oriented programming, where students create and work with classes, objects, and inheritance.

AP Computer Science A culminates in the AP Computer Science A exam, where students showcase their coding prowess and problem-solving abilities through a series of programming tasks. This examination assesses their command over the programming language and their capacity to translate theoretical knowledge into practical applications.

AP Computer Science Principles

In contrast to the more coding-centric approach of AP Computer Science A, AP Computer Science Principles takes a broader and more interdisciplinary approach to computer science education. This course seeks to introduce students to the foundational principles that underpin computer science, emphasizing the following areas:

- Computational thinking: Students develop a computational mindset, which includes skills like abstraction, problem decomposition, pattern recognition, and algorithmic thinking.

- Programming fundamentals: While coding is a component, it is not the sole focus. Students learn the basics of programming but also explore concepts like data analysis and visualization.

- Impact of technology: The course delves into the societal and ethical implications of technology, emphasizing the importance of responsible and ethical use of computer science in a rapidly changing world.

- Creative problem-solving: AP Computer Science Principles encourages students to think creatively and apply their computational knowledge to solve real-world problems, fostering innovation and adaptability.

The assessment for AP Computer Science Principles includes both multiple-choice questions and performance tasks, evaluating not only students' understanding of computer science concepts but also their ability to apply these principles in various contexts.

Recommended Online Course Providers

If your students are seeking additional resources and online courses to supplement their AP studies, there are several to recommend:

- edX: edX offers a wide range of computer science courses, including those related to AP Computer Science A and AP Computer Science Principles.

- Coursera: Coursera provides access to courses from top universities and institutions, offering opportunities to enhance programming and computer science skills.

- Khan Academy: Khan Academy offers free computer science courses that can help students strengthen their foundational knowledge.

- Codecademy: Codecademy provides interactive coding lessons and projects, making it a useful resource for hands-on programming practice.

- edgenuity: Edgenuity offers online courses, including AP Computer Science Principles, that match College Board standards and can be useful for exam preparation.

- Code.org: Code.org is a resource for students interested in computer science and coding. They offer a variety of coding courses and tutorials suitable for all skill levels, including resources aligned with AP Computer Science.

- ProjectSTEM.org: ProjectSTEM.org is platform offering STEM-related courses and resources. They cover various aspects of science, technology, engineering, and mathematics, including topics relevant to AP Computer Science.

Scholarships for Computer Science Students

Scholarships help to empower students to pursue their passions and goals in computer science. Many are available specifically for underrepresented students, tailored to their specific needs. These scholarships are examples of the multitude of those available for people pursuing tech careers. Check for others that may be available in your state.

- The Accenture American Indian Scholarship Fund: The Accenture American Indian Scholarship Fund supports Native American students pursuing degrees in various fields. Applicants must demonstrate American Indian heritage, be enrolled full-time in an accredited institution, maintain a minimum GPA, and display financial need.

- American Indian Science and Engineering Society and Intel Scholarship: This partnership scholarship encourages Native American students to pursue STEM fields, including computer science, by providing financial assistance. Eligible applicants must be members of the American Indian Science and Engineering Society (AISES), have a declared STEM major, and demonstrate academic excellence.

- Blacks at Microsoft Scholarship: This scholarship, sponsored by Microsoft, aims to empower Black students pursuing degrees in computer science and related fields. Applicants must be high school seniors of African descent, pursuing a degree in STEM, and demonstrate leadership abilities.

- ESA Foundation Scholarship: The ESA Foundation Scholarship supports students, including women and minority groups, who are passionate about computer and video game arts. Eligible applicants must be pursuing a career in computer science or related fields, exhibit a strong academic record, and demonstrate a commitment to the video game industry.

- Gates Millennium Scholars Program: Founded by the Bill and Melinda Gates Foundation, this program provides scholarships to underrepresented minority students, including those interested in computer science. Applicants must be high school seniors from minority backgrounds, maintain a minimum GPA, and exhibit leadership and community service involvement.

- GMiS STEM Scholarships: Great Minds in STEM (GMiS) offers scholarships to Hispanic students pursuing STEM degrees. Eligible applicants must be of Hispanic heritage, demonstrate financial need, and have a strong academic record.

- Hispanic Scholarship Fund: The Hispanic Scholarship Fund empowers Hispanic students, including those interested in computer science, by providing scholarships and support. Applicants must be of Hispanic heritage, be U.S. citizens or legal residents, maintain a minimum GPA, and exhibit financial need.

- NACME Minority Scholarships and Engineering Scholarships for Minorities: The National Action Council for Minorities in Engineering (NACME) offers various scholarships to support minority students pursuing engineering and computer science degrees. Eligibility criteria may vary by scholarship, but typically include minority status, academic excellence, and commitment to engineering or computer science.

- EPP/MSI Undergraduate Scholarship Program: The NOAA Educational Partnership Program (EPP) provides scholarships to students pursuing STEM fields at minority-serving institutions. Eligible applicants must attend an MSI, maintain a minimum GPA, and demonstrate an interest in NOAA-related disciplines.

- The Center for Women in Technology at UMBC Scholarship: This scholarship supports women pursuing STEM degrees, including computer science, at the University of Maryland, Baltimore County (UMBC). Eligible applicants must be women, attend UMBC, and demonstrate a commitment to promoting gender diversity in STEM.

- SWE Scholarship: The Society of Women Engineers (SWE) offers scholarships to support women pursuing degrees in STEM fields. Eligible applicants must be women pursuing a STEM degree, exhibit strong academic performance, and demonstrate involvement in SWE.

- Palantir Scholarship for Women in Technology: Palantir Technologies offers scholarships to support women pursuing degrees in technology fields. Applicants must be women, exhibit academic excellence, and demonstrate a passion for technology.

- Buildium Women in Technology Scholarship: Buildium's scholarship program aims to empower women pursuing degrees in technology. Eligible applicants must be women, maintain a minimum GPA, and submit an essay on a technology-related topic.

- Michigan Council of Women in Technology Undergraduate Scholarship: This scholarship supports women pursuing technology-related degrees in the state of Michigan. Applicants must be women, residents of Michigan, and demonstrate academic excellence.

- Women in Defense Scholarships: Women in Defense (WID) offers scholarships to support women pursuing STEM and national security related degrees. Eligibility criteria may vary by scholarship, but typically include women pursuing STEM or national security fields.

Internships for Computer Science Students

Internships offer students a unique opportunity to apply their computer science knowledge in real-world settings, gain practical experience, and explore potential career paths. These are a few you may want your students to consider:

- Google Summer Internship: Google's highly competitive summer internship program provides students with hands-on experience working on projects that impact millions of users worldwide.

- Microsoft Explore Internship: The Microsoft Explore Internship offers students a chance to gain insight into the company's culture and work on meaningful projects across various teams.

- Facebook University for Engineering Internship: Facebook University for Engineering (FBU) is a internship program designed to expose students to software engineering at Facebook.

- Amazon Software Development Engineer Internship: Amazon's internship program allows students to work alongside experienced engineers and tackle challenging technical problems.

- Apple Internship Program: Apple offers internships in software engineering and related fields, allowing students to contribute to innovative projects.

- IBM Extreme Blue Internship: IBM's Extreme Blue program pairs interns with IBM mentors to work on cutting-edge technology projects.

- Intel Internship Program: Intel's internship opportunities span various departments, allowing students to gain experience in areas like hardware design, software engineering, and data science.

- Cisco Internship Program: Cisco's internship program offers students the chance to work on impactful projects and develop their networking and technology skills.

- NVIDIA Internship Program: NVIDIA provides internships in areas such as artificial intelligence, deep learning, and graphics.

- Adobe Internship Program: Adobe offers internships in software engineering, design, and data science, allowing students to contribute to creative and technical projects.

- VMware Internship Program: VMware's internship program focuses on virtualization and cloud computing, offering students opportunities to work on cutting-edge technology.

- Salesforce Internship Program: Salesforce's internships cover various departments, including software engineering and data science, and provide students with hands-on experience.

- Oracle Internship Program: Oracle's internship program offers students the chance to work on cloud technology, databases, and software development.

- Twitter Internship Program: Twitter's internship program allows students to contribute to the company's platform and work on projects related to social media technology.

- Dropbox Internship Program: Dropbox provides internships in software engineering, data science, and product management, among other areas.

- Uber Engineering Internship: Uber's internship program allows students to work on projects related to transportation technology and data science.

- LinkedIn Internship Program: LinkedIn offers internships in software engineering, data science, and product management, helping students build valuable professional connections.

- Yelp Software Engineer Internship: Yelp's internship program focuses on software engineering, allowing students to work on features that impact millions of users.

- Reddit Internship Program: Reddit provides internships in engineering, data science, and product management, allowing students to contribute to the Reddit platform.

- Palantir Internship Program: Palantir's internship program offers students the opportunity to work on projects related to data integration and analysis.

The Range of Careers Available in Computer Science

A degree in computer science opens doors to a vast array of career opportunities, spanning diverse industries and specialties. Let's look at an overview of the various careers in computer science.

Software Developer

Software developers design and create computer programs and applications. They are responsible for translating user needs into functional software solutions. They work closely with stakeholders to understand requirements, write code, and test applications to ensure they meet quality and performance standards. Software developers often work with various programming languages and frameworks.

According to the U.S. Bureau of Labor Statistics, software developers earn an average income of $112,620 per year in the United States.

Data Scientist

Data scientists analyze and interpret complex data to inform decision-making. They use statistical and machine learning techniques to extract insights, trends, and patterns from large datasets. Data scientists play a crucial role in helping organizations make data-driven decisions and solve complex problems.

According to Glassdoor, the average income for data scientists is approximately $96,072 per year.

Cybersecurity Analyst

Cybersecurity analysts protect organizations from cyber threats and breaches. They monitor network and system security, analyze vulnerabilities, and implement security measures to safeguard sensitive information. Cybersecurity analysts are responsible for detecting and responding to security incidents to prevent data breaches and cyberattacks.

The U.S. Bureau of Labor Statistics reports an average income of $76,410 per year for cybersecurity analysts. Cybersecurity professionals with specialized skills and certifications may earn higher salaries.

Machine Learning Engineer

Machine learning engineers design and implement machine learning models and algorithms. They work on developing and deploying machine learning solutions that can make predictions, classify data, or automate tasks. Machine learning engineers need strong programming and data science skills to create effective models.

According to Glassdoor, the average income for machine learning engineers is around $112,000 per year. Experienced machine learning engineers with a track record of successful projects often command higher salaries.

Database Administrator

Database administrators manage and secure databases, ensuring data integrity, availability, and performance. They design and maintain database systems, handle backups and recovery procedures, and implement access controls to protect sensitive data. Database administrators play a critical role in ensuring data reliability and security.

The U.S. Bureau of Labor Statistics reports an average income of $98,860 per year for database administrators. Skilled and certified database administrators may earn higher incomes.

Software Engineer

Software engineers design and develop software applications and systems. They work on writing, testing, and maintaining code to create functional and efficient software solutions. Software engineers collaborate with cross-functional teams to ensure that software meets user requirements and is robust, secure, and scalable.

According to the U.S. Bureau of Labor Statistics, software engineers earn an average income of $112,620 per year in the United States.

Cloud Solutions Architect

Cloud solutions architects design and implement cloud-based infrastructure and services. They work with organizations to plan and build cloud solutions that meet their specific needs. Cloud solutions architects need expertise in cloud platforms like AWS, Azure, or

Google Cloud, and they help organizations leverage cloud technology for scalability, cost-efficiency, and flexibility.

PayScale reports an average income of approximately $116,351 per year for cloud solutions architects.

Full Stack Developer

Full stack developers work on both front-end and back-end components of web applications. They are proficient in a variety of programming languages and technologies, allowing them to develop and maintain all aspects of a web application. Full stack developers are responsible for creating seamless and user-friendly web experiences.

According to Glassdoor, the average income for full stack developers is around $80,000 per year.

Game Developer

Game developers create interactive video games for various platforms. They are responsible for designing game mechanics, graphics, audio, and gameplay features. Game developers may specialize in areas like game design, 3D modeling, or game programming.

The U.S. Bureau of Labor Statistics reports an average income of $75,770 per year for game developers.

Mobile App Developer

Mobile app developers design and develop applications for smartphones and tablets. They work on both Android and iOS platforms, creating user-friendly and functional mobile apps. Mobile app developers are proficient in programming languages like Java, Swift, or Kotlin.

According to PayScale, the average income for mobile app developers is approximately $73,694 per year.

DevOps Engineer

DevOps engineers focus on automating and streamlining software development and deployment processes. They bridge the gap between development and operations teams, ensuring faster and more reliable software delivery. DevOps engineers use tools and practices to enhance collaboration and efficiency.

Glassdoor reports an average income of about $94,594 per year for DevOps engineers.

Network Engineer

Network engineers design and manage computer networks and infrastructure. They ensure network reliability, security, and performance. Network engineers are responsible for configuring routers, switches, and firewalls, as well as troubleshooting network issues.

PayScale reports an average income of approximately $93,251 per year for network engineers.

Web Developer

Web developers create and maintain websites and web applications. They work on the front end, back end, or full stack of web development, using languages like HTML, CSS, JavaScript, and various web frameworks.

The U.S. Bureau of Labor Statistics reports an average income of $73,760 per year for web developers.

AI Research Scientist

AI research scientists conduct research and develop artificial intelligence technologies. They work on cutting-edge AI projects, including natural language processing, computer vision, and machine learning. AI research scientists often publish research papers and collaborate with academia and industry.

PayScale reports an average income of approximately $124,341 per year for AI research scientists.

Quality Assurance Analyst

Quality assurance analysts test software and applications to ensure they meet quality standards. They identify and report bugs, create test plans, and work closely with developers to resolve issues. Quality assurance analysts play a crucial role in delivering reliable and error-free software.

According to Glassdoor, the average income for quality assurance analysts is approximately $60,342 per year.

IT Project Manager

IT project managers oversee technology projects, ensuring they are delivered on time and within budget. They develop project plans, allocate resources, and manage teams to meet project goals. IT project managers play a critical role in ensuring the successful execution of technology initiatives.

The U.S. Bureau of Labor Statistics reports an average income of $93,250 per year for IT project managers.

Computer and Information Research Scientist

Computer and information research scientists conduct research to advance computing technologies. They explore new algorithms, software, and hardware innovations. Their work often leads to breakthroughs in areas like artificial intelligence, cybersecurity, and data science.

The U.S. Bureau of Labor Statistics reports an average income of $126,830 per year for computer and information research scientists.

IT Consultant

IT consultants provide expertise and solutions to organizations to improve their IT infrastructure. They assess technology needs, recommend solutions, and implement strategies to enhance efficiency and productivity. IT consultants often work on a project basis with various clients.

PayScale reports an average income of approximately $88,386 per year for IT consultants.

UI/UX Designer

UI/UX designers create user-friendly interfaces and improve user experiences in software and apps. They focus on designing intuitive and visually appealing interfaces that enhance user satisfaction. UI/UX designers collaborate with developers to ensure the seamless integration of design and functionality.

Glassdoor reports an average income of about $81,222 per year for UI/UX designers.

Computer Hardware Engineer

Computer hardware engineers design and develop computer hardware components. They work on creating CPUs, GPUs, motherboards, and other hardware components. Computer hardware engineers ensure that computer systems operate efficiently and reliably.

The U.S. Bureau of Labor Statistics reports an average income of $119,560 per year for computer hardware engineers.

Business Intelligence Analyst

Business intelligence analysts use data to inform business decisions and strategies. They gather and analyze data from various sources, create reports and dashboards, and provide insights to help organizations make informed choices and optimize their operations.

According to Glassdoor, the average income for business intelligence analysts is approximately $75,403 per year.

In an ideal world, inequality in computer science wouldn't be an issue. Unfortunately, even when teachers increase diversity in the classroom, students will need to develop some grit to gain confidence, fight for the cause, and become advocates for diversity. In the next chapter, you will discover how to empower your students to become such advocates.

Chapter 10:

Empowering Students to Make a Difference

It is everyone's responsibility to speak up and speak out. Equitable opportunities and outcomes for all are goals we all must embrace and promote.
–Fay Beydoun

This chapter will focus on passing on the diversity torch. You will discover ways to inspire your students to make positive changes for future classes and even reach out to help others who are interested in technology but don't have the confidence to start. They can become role models, themselves.

Helping Underrepresented Students Develop Confidence

Confidence is a major factor in the success of underrepresented students in both educational settings and the workforce. Building confidence involves nurturing traits like resilience, empathy, emotional intelligence, and strong communication skills. These skills collectively contribute to a student's grit, their determination to overcome challenges and embrace growth opportunities.

Embracing Challenges

Grit and resilience are closely intertwined with the concept of a growth mindset. This mindset encourages students to perceive challenges and failures not as insurmountable obstacles but as valuable lessons. It shifts their perspective from a fixed belief in innate abilities to the understanding that intelligence and skills can be developed through effort and learning. You have the important role of creating an environment where setbacks are viewed as valuable learning experiences. By destigmatizing failure and emphasizing its role in the learning process, you help your students develop healthier relationships with challenges. This, in turn, boosts their confidence in their ability to overcome obstacles.

Comfort Zone Expansion

A great way to help students develop grit and resilience is by encouraging underrepresented students to step outside their comfort zones. This can manifest in various forms, such as participating in extracurricular activities, taking on leadership roles, or challenging themselves with advanced coursework. Some of the ways you can do this include:

- Extracurricular engagement: Extracurricular activities provide an ideal platform for students to explore new interests, develop skills, and build confidence. Whether it's joining a club, sports team, or community service group, students broaden their horizons and gain exposure to diverse experiences.

- Leadership opportunities: Taking on leadership roles allows students to push their boundaries and take ownership of their educational journeys. Whether it's leading a project, organizing an event, or mentoring peers, assuming leadership responsibilities instills a sense of purpose and self-assurance.

- Advanced coursework: Tackling advanced coursework challenges students to improve their academic performance. While it may initially seem daunting, success in advanced courses reinforces the belief that they can excel in demanding academic environments.

The Teacher's Role

You serve as a guide and mentor in this process, helping your students build their grit and resilience by:

- Creating a supportive environment: You can establish a classroom environment where students feel safe to take risks, make mistakes, and grow from them. Encourage open dialogue and provide constructive feedback.

- Setting realistic expectations: Setting achievable yet challenging goals helps students build confidence as they progress. You can help students set milestones and celebrate their accomplishments along the way.

- Fostering perseverance: You can emphasize the value of perseverance by sharing stories of famous individuals who faced adversity but persevered to achieve success. These stories serve as inspiration and proof that grit can lead to remarkable accomplishments.

- Mentoring and support: Providing mentorship and support, both academically and emotionally, is important. You can be a trusted ally who guides students through their education, offering advice, encouragement, and resources when needed.

Empathy and Emotional Intelligence

Empathy and emotional intelligence are qualities that contribute to an inclusive and compassionate society. These qualities enable people to connect with others on a deeper level, create a sense of belonging, and navigate interpersonal relationships with sensitivity and understanding.

Cultivating Empathy

Empathy involves the ability to understand and share the feelings, perspectives, and experiences of others. You can nurture empathy by creating an environment where students are encouraged to share their own stories, viewpoints, and backgrounds. By actively listening to each other's narratives, students develop a greater understanding of the diverse world around them.

Encouraging empathy among students develops inclusivity and a sense of belonging within the classroom. When students learn to appreciate the unique qualities and perspectives of their peers, the way is paved for unity among diverse groups. You can facilitate activities that promote empathy, such as group discussions, storytelling, or collaborative projects that require students to see issues from multiple angles.

Emotional Intelligence

Emotional intelligence involves recognizing, understanding, and effectively managing one's own emotions. It also extends to empathizing with the emotions of others. You can introduce emotional intelligence education into the curriculum, helping students develop self-awareness and interpersonal skills.

Emotional intelligence begins with self-awareness. Educators can guide students in exploring their emotions, helping them identify and understand their feelings. This self-reflection empowers students to manage their emotions in a healthy and constructive way.

Teaching students how to interact effectively with others is a core component of emotional intelligence. This includes understanding the emotional cues of peers, empathizing with their experiences, and communicating with sensitivity. Role-playing exercises and group activities can help students practice these skills.

The Teacher's Role

You can play a central role in nurturing empathy and emotional intelligence among your students by:

- Creating a supportive environment: You can create a classroom environment where students feel safe to express their emotions and discuss their feelings. Encouraging open dialogue allows students to share their experiences and perspectives without fear of judgment.

- Modeling empathy: You serve as a role model by demonstrating empathy in your interactions with students. You can do this by actively listening, validating students' emotions, and showing understanding and support.

- Curricular integration: Incorporating empathy-building activities and emotional intelligence lessons into the curriculum helps students develop these skills systematically. This can include reading literature that explores diverse perspectives, discussing real-world issues, and engaging in mindfulness practices.

- Conflict resolution: You can teach conflict resolution strategies that draw on emotional intelligence, helping students navigate disagreements and misunderstandings in a constructive and empathetic manner.

Strong Communication Skills

Strong communication skills help to develop confidence and empowerment in both academic settings and future careers. These skills enable your students to express themselves effectively, engage in meaningful dialogue, and navigate diverse environments. Let's look at how you can develop these skills in your students.

Effective Communication

Public speaking is a great tool for building confidence. You can create opportunities for underrepresented students to practice speaking in front of their peers. Activities like class presentations, debates, or storytelling sessions not only enhance communication skills but also boost students' self-assurance.

Encouraging students to articulate their thoughts clearly is important for effective communication. You can provide guidance on structuring ideas, using appropriate vocabulary, and organizing information logically. As students become more proficient in conveying their thoughts, they gain confidence in their ability to express themselves.

You can model respectful communication and encourage students to express differing opinions in a considerate and empathetic manner. This helps build a classroom culture of open and inclusive communication.

Active Listening

Active listening is a vital component of strong communication. It involves not only hearing but also comprehending and responding to what others are saying. You can teach students active listening by providing guidelines on maintaining eye contact, nodding to show understanding, and paraphrasing to confirm comprehension.

Encouraging students to actively engage in discussions and ask questions develops their confidence in their ability to contribute meaningfully to conversations. When students feel that their voices are heard and valued, they become more confident communicators.

The Teacher's Role

You play a pivotal role in nurturing strong communication skills in your students by:

- Creating a supportive environment: Establish a classroom environment where students feel safe to express themselves without fear of judgment. Encourage open and respectful communication.

- Modeling effective communication: You can serve as a role model by demonstrating effective communication in your interactions with students. They can actively listen, ask clarifying questions, and provide constructive feedback.

- Structured communication opportunities: Adding structured communication opportunities into the curriculum allows students to practice and refine their skills. This can include debates, group discussions, peer presentations, or collaborative projects that require communication.

- Peer feedback: Encouraging peer feedback allows students to learn from each other and refine their communication skills. Students can provide constructive feedback on each other's presentations or communication styles.

Welcoming Environment and Cultural Understanding

Creating a welcoming environment and promoting cultural understanding are foundational to building confidence in underrepresented students. These encourage students to embrace their unique backgrounds and identities while having a sense of belonging within the school community.

Celebrating Differences

A welcoming environment begins with actively promoting diversity and inclusion. Schools should emphasize that every student's background and perspective is valuable. This can be achieved through events, programs, and curricula that highlight different cultures, traditions, and experiences. Celebrating differences helps students feel acknowledged and valued. When students see their own cultures and identities celebrated in the school environment, it gives them a sense of belonging. This sense of belonging is a core component of building confidence, as it assures students that their unique backgrounds are not only accepted but celebrated.

Cultural Competence

Take the time to learn about the cultures of underrepresented students in your classrooms. Understanding their backgrounds, traditions, and experiences helps build trust and rapport. It also helps you to create culturally responsive teaching strategies that resonate with your students.

Adding diverse perspectives and voices into the curriculum is a great way to demonstrate cultural competence. This allows students to see themselves represented in their learning materials and fosters a deeper connection to the subject matter.

Positive Self-Talk and Advocacy

Positive self-talk and advocacy are essential in nurturing the confidence of your students. These aspects encourage students to cultivate belief in themselves, challenge negative self-perceptions, and actively advocate for their success.

Encouraging Positive Self-Talk

Self-talk plays a massive role in building confidence. You can teach underrepresented students to recognize and challenge negative self-perceptions. Encouraging self-affirmations, self-belief, and a growth mindset will help them develop a positive self-image. Emphasizing the power of a growth mindset reinforces the idea that abilities and skills can be developed through effort and learning. Students who believe in their potential are more likely to persevere through challenges and build confidence.

Advocacy for Success

You can be a powerful advocate for your students. This advocacy goes beyond academic support and extends to addressing any barriers or biases that underrepresented students may face. By actively advocating for your students' needs, you ensure that their voices are heard and their challenges are addressed.

You can also empower underrepresented students to become advocates for themselves. Encouraging students to speak up, ask for support when needed, and assert their rights builds their confidence in their ability to succeed.

The Teacher's Role

You can play a central role in creating a welcoming environment, promoting cultural understanding, and encouraging positive self-talk and advocacy by:

- Creating inclusive classrooms: You can design classrooms that reflect and celebrate diversity. You can integrate multicultural perspectives into lessons, showcase students' cultural contributions, and create an atmosphere where everyone feels valued.

- Supporting students: Providing support and mentorship helps underrepresented students navigate the challenges they may encounter.

- Promoting self-advocacy skills: You can teach students how to advocate for themselves effectively. This includes helping them develop the skills to articulate their needs, seek help when necessary, and assert themselves in academic and social settings.

Examples of Students Fighting for Classroom Diversity

Students across the United States have for a while been advocating for classroom diversity, equity, and inclusion. These passionate young activists are driving change by challenging existing systems and pushing for more inclusive educational experiences. By teaching your students about them, you can encourage the next generation of advocates.

Diversify Our Narrative

Diversify Our Narrative is a nationwide organization comprising over 6,000 students who are committed to fighting against anti-racist tests in U.S. schools. Their mission extends beyond standardized tests. They also advocate for racially diverse literature, curricula, and teaching practices. They aim to reshape educational landscapes to be more inclusive and equitable.

Inclusive Excellence at Colorado State University

Inclusive Excellence at Colorado State University is an initiative that proactively seeks to build a more inclusive community. This comprehensive effort encompasses changes to codes of conduct, diversity training, mental health support, reporting mechanisms for bias incidents, and improvements in security and safety. Students play a role in driving these changes, advocating for a campus environment that values diversity and equity.

Diversity & Inclusion Student Advocates at Brown University

At Brown University, the Diversity & Inclusion Student Advocates focus on increasing the representation of historically underrepresented groups in upper-level computer science courses. By advocating for equitable access to educational opportunities and addressing barriers to inclusion, these students strive to make computer science education more diverse and accessible.

Holt High School Student Activists

At Holt High School in Holt, Michigan, a dedicated group of student activists is working diligently to increase the diversity among teachers. Recognizing the importance of having a teaching staff that reflects the diversity of the student body, these students engage in activism efforts to bring about meaningful change within their school community.

Inspiring Students to Become Advocates for Diversity

Empowering your students to become advocates for diversity is a step toward creating a more inclusive and equitable society. You can nurture your students' passion for activism and foster a commitment to social justice. Let's look at how you can help your students become advocates.

- Create a safe space: Establish a classroom environment where students feel safe to express their thoughts and engage in discussions about diversity and social justice.

- Encourage critical thinking: Foster critical thinking skills by encouraging students to question, analyze, and evaluate information related to diversity issues.

- Provide resources: Offer access to diverse literature, films, and resources that allow students to explore various perspectives and cultures.

- Promote dialogue: Facilitate open and respectful discussions about diversity and inclusion, encouraging students to share their experiences and insights.

- Teach empathy: Incorporate empathy-building activities that help students understand and appreciate different viewpoints and life experiences.

- Support student initiatives: Encourage and support students' ideas for promoting diversity and equity within the school community.

- Cultivate leadership: Provide opportunities for students to take on leadership roles in diversity-related initiatives and projects.

- Collaborate with communities: Partner with local organizations and community leaders to engage students in real-world diversity and inclusion efforts.

- Celebrate achievements: Acknowledge and celebrate the positive impact that student-led diversity initiatives have on the school and community.

Ideas for Students to Fight for Diversity

Your students can become advocates by doing the following:

- Organize diversity workshops: Students can collaborate with teachers and administrators to plan and host diversity workshops that address relevant issues, encourage dialogue, and promote understanding among peers.

- Start a diversity club: Initiate a student-led diversity club or affinity group focused on celebrating and advocating for diversity within the school community.

- Campaign for inclusive curricula: Advocate for more inclusive and diverse curricula by petitioning school boards, administrators, and educators to incorporate diverse perspectives and voices into coursework.

- Peer education: Students can become peer educators by organizing presentations or workshops on diversity topics for their peers, sharing knowledge and fostering empathy.

- Awareness campaigns: Launch awareness campaigns that address stereotypes, biases, and microaggressions within the school environment. Use posters, social media, or awareness events to reach a broader audience.

- Promote inclusive events: Collaborate with school clubs and organizations to ensure that events and activities are inclusive and celebrate diverse cultures, traditions, and backgrounds.

- Advocate for diverse faculty: Encourage schools to actively recruit and retain a diverse teaching staff to better reflect the student body's diversity.

- Participate in community outreach: Engage in community service projects that promote diversity and inclusion, such as volunteering at local cultural festivals or supporting organizations dedicated to these causes.

- Support inclusive policies: Advocate for school policies and practices that promote equity and inclusivity, such as gender-neutral restrooms, inclusive dress codes, or anti-bullying initiatives.

- Collaborate with existing initiatives: Join or collaborate with existing diversity and inclusion initiatives, such as those mentioned in previous sections, to amplify their impact and contribute to their success.

Some minority groups will undoubtedly have financial obstacles that could prevent them from moving forward with their career in computer science. In the final chapter, we will take a closer look at AP credits and how these can be advantageous for future placement.

Chapter 11:

Earning College Credits: AP Courses and Cal State Schools

Through our Redesigning the Student Experience process, we were able to truly center equity and design cross-functional Student Success Teams to support our first-time college students that were disproportionately impacted.
–Luke Lara

The focus of this chapter is for you to understand how AP credits work and the benefits of attaining credits, specifically for California State University. While the main focus will be on Cal State schools, there will be guidance on policies for other schools and programs within computer sciences.

Unlocking the Value of Advanced Placement Courses

For high school students, Advanced Placement courses present a unique opportunity to engage in college-level coursework, opening doors to academic enrichment, cost savings, and an accelerated path to graduation. Let's look at AP credits so we can understand how they work, their intrinsic value, and the impact they can have on your students' college life.

Understanding the Mechanics of AP Credits

AP courses are crafted to challenge high school students with the academic rigor and content characteristic of college-level coursework. These courses span a diverse spectrum of subjects, encompassing mathematics, science, humanities, and the even arts. When students enroll in an AP course, they are granted the opportunity to earn AP credits based on their performance throughout the course.

Each AP course typically carries a specified credit weight, often equating to the value of a college course. Most AP courses merit either three or four college credits, contingent on the course's depth, intensity, and academic scope.

The primary advantage of amassing AP credits lies in the potential to bypass specific college prerequisites or requirements. This shortcut allows students to accelerate through their college curriculum, affording them the freedom to select courses aligned with their interests and potentially expediting the time—and expense—necessary for degree completion.

Cost Considerations: Participation in an AP course and the associated exam typically costs approximately $96. However, fee reductions or waivers may be available for students with financial constraints. The College Board, the organization responsible for administering AP exams, offers detailed information regarding eligibility for fee reductions and the application process to help students in need.

Varied Value

The potential number of college credits attainable through Advanced Placement courses is contingent on the specific AP course and the policies of the college or university they choose to attend. This determines the value of their AP credits.

How many college credits a student can earn hinges on the specific AP course they undertake. The intricacy, depth, and breadth of the subject matter in the course serves as the chief arbiter. Some AP courses have a heightened level of complexity, warranting them four college credits, whereas others are accorded three credits.

The second determinant is the policies laid out by the college or university where the student plans to pursue higher education. Each institution establishes its own set of guidelines governing the acceptance and allocation of AP credits. Some colleges accept AP credits exclusively for designated courses or as elective credits. Other institutions may permit AP credits to fulfill general education prerequisites. Your students will want to do research into their preferred colleges before choosing AP courses.

AP Courses and California State Schools

For students and parents in California, or for those planning on studying there, Advanced Placement courses offer an excellent opportunity to supplement high school education, earn college credits, and potentially reduce the cost and time associated with higher education. The College Board provides a wealth of resources for students and parents in California.

College Board resources include the AP Course Search tool to help students find AP courses offered at their high schools. The AP Credit Policy search tool allows students to check how colleges and universities in California and across the United States accept AP credits.

The College Board website also offers information on fee reductions for students facing financial difficulties. Also look into the AP Capstone Diploma Program, which offers advanced research and writing opportunities for students.

The Next Step to California State University, Los Angeles (Cal State LA)

California State University, Los Angeles (often shortened to Cal State LA) is an excellent choice for students interested in pursuing computer science education, thanks to its commitment to diversity and a comprehensive range of programs.

The Computer Science Department has been recognized for its commitment to diversity, earning the bronze award by the American Society for Engineering Education (ASEE) Diversity Recognition program. This recognition shows the department's dedication to creating an inclusive and diverse learning environment.

Cal State LA offers a bachelor of science in Computer Science, preparing students for careers in various technology-related fields. The program covers fundamental computer science principles and provides hands-on experience.

Cal State LA also offers integrated programs that allow students to earn both their bachelor's and master's degrees in a shorter time frame. The department offers integrated programs in computer science for eligible students looking to accelerate their education.

The Computer Science Department offers master of science programs in computer science and software engineering. These programs offer advanced coursework and research opportunities for students seeking graduate-level education.

Cal State LA also offers minors in computer science, allowing students from various majors to gain valuable computer science skills.

Student Objectives and Vision Statement

The Computer Science Department at Cal State LA has defined clear student objectives and a vision statement to guide its educational mission.

Student Objectives

- To provide students with a strong foundation in computer science principles and practices.

- To prepare students for successful careers in the computing industry or further advanced studies.

- To foster critical thinking, problem-solving skills, and adaptability in students.

- To nurture a commitment to ethical and responsible computing practices.

- To promote diversity and inclusivity within the computer science field.

Vision Statement

The Department of Computer Science strives to be a recognized leader in computer science education and research, fostering excellence and innovation in teaching, research, and community engagement. We are committed to providing a diverse, equitable, and inclusive learning environment that empowers our students to excel as computer science professionals and global citizens.

Additional Resources

Cal State LA's Computer Science Department offers various resources, including job and internship opportunities, to help students bridge the gap between education and industry experience. These resources provide hands-on experience and networking opportunities for students preparing to enter the tech workforce. Above this, a wealth of computer science resources is available to improve teaching and learning. Let's look at list of resources for both teachers and students of all ages:

CSforCA Resources

CSforCA is an organization working to advance computer science education in California. Their resources section offers a wide range of materials, lesson plans, and tools for teachers, students, and parents.

Explore this website and sign up for updates to stay informed about the latest developments in computer science education in California.

Ellipsis Education

Ellipsis Education provides a curated list of resources and programs related to computer science education in California. It's a valuable source for educators looking for teaching materials and opportunities. Consider signing up for newsletters or updates to stay connected.

Computer Science Equity Project

The Computer Science Equity Project at UCLA aims to promote equitable access to computer science education. Their website offers insights, research, and resources for educators striving to make computer science more inclusive.

California K-12 Computer Science Standards

The state's computer science standards outline the expectations for computer science education in California at different grade levels. They provide a valuable framework for educators to develop and align their computer science curriculum. You can review these standards to make sure your teaching materials align with California's educational goals.

California Department of Education Alerts

California's Department of Education alerts provide essential information and updates on education-related topics, including computer science. Subscribing to these alerts ensures that teachers receive timely notifications about changes and opportunities in the field.

Access California

Access California is an organization dedicated to advancing computer science education. Their mission is to provide opportunities and support for all students to learn computer science. Explore the resources and initiatives offered by Access California and consider participating in their programs.

Besides exploring these websites, you can actively engage with the computer science education community in California. This involvement can include attending workshops, joining professional organizations, collaborating with colleagues, and participating in advocacy efforts. By staying informed and actively contributing to the field, you can play a role in advancing computer science education in the state and ensuring that students have access to high-quality learning experiences.

That's it for this chapter, but remember to check out the conclusion and the glossary, which is packed full of useful definitions you can use to simplify computer science terms in your classroom.

Thanks for reading!

Conclusion

Throughout this book we have discovered how to foster diversity and inclusion in computer science education. As we reach the end, let us reiterate the vital message at its core: diversity in computer science is not merely an option but a necessity, and it must begin from the earliest stages of education.

The tech industry's lack of diversity remains a persistent challenge, one deeply rooted in systemic issues and historical disparities. To bridge this gap, we have learned that intervention must commence as early as kindergarten, planting the seeds of diversity and inclusion in young minds. Why? Because every child, regardless of their background, deserves the opportunity to thrive. Inclusivity is the future of computer science.

I implore you to take action. It's time to assess your own classroom to ask whether it truly embodies inclusivity. If not, engage your students, for they are the future. Positive transformations begin within the classroom walls, and by working together, we can forge a brighter future for all.

In closing, I urge you to share your insights and experiences by leaving a review on Amazon. Let your fellow educators learn from your wisdom and join the mission to prioritize diversity in computer science education. Remember, the path to a more inclusive world is one we must walk hand in hand, and together, we can unlock opportunities for all!

About the Author

Jordan B. Smith Jr., a trailblazing educator and military veteran, was born in St. Louis, Missouri, and his journey has included a series of remarkable firsts. He embarked on his academic path at Lexington Grade School and then moved on to the distinguished Christian Brothers College Military Institute, a private school in Clayton, Missouri, where he attended from 1968 to 1972.

During his time at Christian Brothers College Military Institute, Jordan became the first African American to attain the prestigious rank of cadet lieutenant colonel. His extraordinary leadership abilities were further recognized when he became the first African American recipient of the Damian Saber Award for Military Leadership upon graduation. These achievements led to his nomination and appointment to the U.S. Naval Academy in Annapolis, Maryland, in 1972.

At the U.S. Naval Academy, Jordan continued to break new ground, becoming the first African American to hold the esteemed position of 17th Color Company commander in June of 1976. His appointment to this role was a historic moment in the academy's history, symbolizing his commitment to excellence and dedication to leadership. During his tenure, he had the honor of selecting the first and only African American Color Girl for the Color Parade in June 1976, marking the end of an all-male parade era.

Upon graduation, Jordan was commissioned as a 2nd lieutenant in the U.S. Marine Corps, embarking on a remarkable 20-year career as a logistics officer, which included serving in the Gulf War (1990-1991) with Marine Air Group 26 (MAG-26). His service to his country was marked by dedication and honor.

Transitioning to the world of education, Jordan has spent over 19 years as a public school mathematics teacher in the San Jacinto Unified School District in Southern California. His passion for teaching led him to earn a master's in secondary education (2006), a doctorate in educational leadership with a specialization in curriculum and instruction (2015), and a master's in administration and services credential (2017).

For the past decade, Jordan has dedicated his efforts to three different alternative schools on the same campus, where he works tirelessly to help at-risk students recover credits and earn their high school diplomas. His deep understanding of mathematics as a roadblock for many students led him to develop unique and effective strategies to motivate and instill confidence in math concepts. Under his guidance, graduation rates have seen remarkable improvements, and students are now recruited to serve in the armed forces of the United States every year.

Beyond the classroom, Jordan has emerged as a multifaceted education leader, public speaker, conference presenter, and educational consultant. He is also an accomplished author, having penned five books, including the recent bestsellers *11 Effective Strategies for Teaching Math to Students Who Have Given Up on Learning,* and *Annapolis Creed: Why Teacher Leaders Like Me Matter.*

In recognition of his unwavering commitment to promoting access to computer science courses, including Advance Placement, for underrepresented groups of students, Jordan was honored as the Amazon Future Engineer Teacher of the Year for 2023. This prestigious award celebrates his role in helping students from underserved and underrepresented communities discover the vast possibilities that computer science and robotics offer for their future.

As part of this recognition, Jordan received a grant of $25,000 from Amazon to expand computer science and robotics education at his school, along with an additional $5,000 cash award. His tireless advocacy for underrepresented groups in technology aligns with the mission to bridge the diversity gap in the computing sector, where women, African Americans, Hispanics, and Native Americans have historically been underrepresented.

Jordan's journey into computer science started early, with exposure to programming during his time at the U.S. Naval Academy in 1972, where computer science became a mandatory course. He later leveraged his programming skills in various roles throughout his career, from the military to teaching. His dedication to technology and innovation made him an ideal candidate to introduce programing solutions in various settings.

Throughout his career, Jordan's commitment to technology extended to roles as a webmaster, instructor, and a proponent of educational technology integration. His knowledge of computers played a pivotal role in facilitating remote learning during the COVID-19 pandemic, ensuring that underrepresented students continued their education despite challenges.

In his quest to make computer science education accessible to all, Jordan attended training in 2021 to teach AP Computer Science Principles, even at an alternative high school where such courses were previously unavailable due to credit deficiencies and other issues. His efforts paid off as students from diverse backgrounds, including those from socioeconomically disadvantaged families, successfully completed the curriculum and took the AP exam.

Building on this success, Jordan further expanded his impact by becoming certified to teach the capstone course AP Computer Science A in the summer of 2022. He introduced over 90 students to computer science during the 2022-2023 school year, with several students achieving success on the AP CSP exam.

Notably, Jordan's commitment to increasing diversity in computer science education extended to independent study students, making it possible for them to take AP courses remotely. This innovative approach broke new ground in the school district, demonstrating that students from underrepresented backgrounds were fully capable of excelling in computer science.

Recognizing the transformative potential of the Amazon Future Engineer program, Jordan used the award money to purchase equipment, expand programming offerings, and enhance the learning experience for his students. As a result, computer science programs are now offered at all three schools within the alternative high school, and the comprehensive high school in the district followed suit.

Jordan's next ambitious goal is to secure scholarships from the Amazon Future Engineer Scholarships program for his students, enabling them to pursue computer science degrees and gain valuable real-world experience as software engineers at Amazon facilities. This opportunity promises to be a life-changing moment for countless underrepresented students and their families.

Jordan B. Smith Jr. is an exceptional educator and advocate who has dedicated his life to breaking down barriers and empowering underrepresented students in the fields of mathematics and computer science. His contributions have not only transformed the lives of individual students but have also helped bridge the diversity gap in technology, making a lasting impact on education and the tech industry. His journey is a testament to the power of determination, innovation, and unwavering commitment to change.

Glossary

Access Equity: Ensuring that all underprivileged students have equal opportunities to access quality computer science education, regardless of their geographical location or school district.

Access to Technology: Providing underprivileged students with the necessary hardware and software tools, such as computers and internet access, to participate in computer science learning.

Accessibility Tools: Software, hardware, and design practices that make technology and digital content accessible to individuals with disabilities.

Advocacy: Promoting and supporting diversity and inclusion efforts, often through active and vocal support for underrepresented groups and challenging discriminatory practices.

Affinity Groups: Groups within an organization or community where individuals with shared backgrounds or identities come together to support each other and promote diversity and inclusion.

All-Inclusive: A term indicating the comprehensive inclusion of individuals from all backgrounds, regardless of their demographic characteristics or identities.

Amazon Awards: A reference to Amazon's recognition of individuals and projects in the field of computer science, highlighting achievements and contributions from diverse sources.

Bias Mitigation Strategies: Techniques and practices aimed at reducing bias in algorithms, AI systems, and technology to ensure fairness and equity.

Bias-Free Algorithms: Algorithms and machine learning models designed to minimize bias and discrimination, especially in applications like hiring and lending.

Community Engagement: Involving local communities and parents in supporting and advocating for computer science education for underprivileged students, creating a network of support.

Community of Educators: A collective group of teachers, instructors, and educators who share knowledge, experiences, and resources to support diversity and inclusion efforts in computer science education.

Community-Based Learning: Educational programs that integrate computer science education with community service and real-world applications, enhancing the relevance and impact of learning for underprivileged students.

Computer Science Education: The process of imparting knowledge and skills related to computer science, including programming, algorithms, and computational thinking, to students from underprivileged backgrounds.

Computer Science for All (CSforAll): An initiative advocating for universal access to computer science education in K-12 schools, with a focus on reaching underprivileged and underrepresented students.

Computer Science Pipeline: The educational path that individuals follow from early exposure to computer science concepts to pursuing advanced degrees and careers in the field.

Cultural Competence: The ability to interact effectively with people from diverse cultural backgrounds, which is essential for educators working with underprivileged students.

Cultural Competency Training: Programs and workshops designed to enhance educators' and professionals' understanding of various cultures and their ability to work effectively with diverse groups.

Cultural Sensitivity: Being aware of and respectful toward cultural differences, which is crucial for creating an inclusive learning environment.

Culturally Relevant Curriculum: Educational materials and content that reflect the cultural backgrounds, experiences, and identities of underprivileged students, making the subject matter more relatable and engaging.

Curriculum Diversification: The process of incorporating diverse perspectives, contributions, and examples into computer science curriculum materials to make them more inclusive.

Cybersecurity Awareness: Educating students, especially underprivileged ones, about online security threats, privacy, and responsible digital behavior.

Digital Citizenship: Teaching students responsible and ethical behavior online, including topics like cyberbullying prevention and online privacy.

Digital Divide Solutions: Strategies and initiatives, such as subsidized internet access and community technology centers, designed to address the digital divide and provide access to technology for underprivileged individuals.

Digital Divide: The gap in access to technology, internet connectivity, and digital resources between different socioeconomic groups, which can affect underprivileged students' access to computer science education.

Digital Equity: A broader term encompassing not only access to technology but also the fair distribution of its benefits and opportunities.

Digital Inclusion: Efforts to bridge the digital divide by ensuring that underprivileged individuals have access to technology and the skills and knowledge to use it effectively.

Digital Literacy: The ability to use technology effectively, including basic computer skills and online safety practices, which is essential for underprivileged students to benefit from computer science education.

Digital Mentorship: Online mentoring relationships between experienced tech professionals and underprivileged students or individuals aspiring to enter the tech field.

Digital Skills Gap: The disparity between the skills needed in the modern workforce, which often include computer science skills, and the skills possessed by underprivileged students, creating barriers to employment and economic mobility.

Digital Storytelling: Using digital media and technology to tell personal stories and narratives, which can be a powerful tool for self-expression and empowerment for underprivileged students.

Diverse Perspectives: Recognizing that individuals from different backgrounds can bring unique insights and problem-solving approaches to computer science and technology.

Diversity and Inclusion Officer: An individual within an organization responsible for leading and overseeing efforts to promote diversity and inclusion, including in computer science education.

Diversity: The presence of individuals from a variety of backgrounds, including but not limited to race, ethnicity, gender, socioeconomic status, disability, and cultural heritage.

Early Intervention: The practice of addressing diversity and inclusion issues in computer science education from the earliest stages of a student's academic journey, including kindergarten and elementary school.

Educational Technology (EdTech): The use of technology, such as software and online platforms, to enhance and support educational processes, including computer science education.

Empowerment: Encouraging underprivileged students to develop self-confidence, skills, and a growth mindset, enabling them to overcome challenges and excel in computer science.

Equity: The principle of ensuring fairness and equal opportunities for all students, irrespective of their backgrounds, by addressing systemic disadvantages and providing necessary support.

Hackathons: Events where participants collaboratively work on computer programming and software development projects, which can promote diversity and skill development in computer science.

Historical Disparities: Inequalities and disadvantages that have persisted over time, often resulting from discriminatory policies, practices, and societal norms.

Implicit Bias: Unconscious attitudes or stereotypes that influence our actions and decisions, often leading to unintentional discrimination.

Inclusion: The active effort to create an environment where diverse individuals are welcomed, respected, and provided with equal opportunities to participate and succeed.

Inclusive Classroom Environment: A learning space where all students, regardless of their backgrounds, feel safe, respected, and valued, and where their diverse perspectives are embraced.

Inclusive Design: The practice of designing products, websites, and technology with a focus on accessibility and usability for people of all abilities and backgrounds.

Inclusive Future: The envisioned outcome of efforts to promote diversity and inclusion in computer science education, where equal opportunities and representation are the norm, leading to innovation and progress in the tech industry.

Inclusive Hiring Practices: Strategies used by employers to ensure diversity and eliminate bias in their hiring processes, including blind resume reviews and diverse interview panels.

Inclusive Language: Using language that is respectful and inclusive of all individuals, regardless of their background or identity, to foster a welcoming and respectful environment.

Inclusive Pedagogy: Teaching methods and strategies that accommodate diverse learning needs and styles, ensuring that all students, including those from underprivileged groups, can participate and succeed.

Inclusivity Awareness: Raising awareness among educators and policymakers about the importance of diversity and inclusion in computer science education and the specific needs of underprivileged students.

Innovation Incubators: Programs and spaces that support underrepresented entrepreneurs and startups in the tech industry by providing resources, mentorship, and networking opportunities.

Intersectional Curriculum: Curriculum materials that consider the intersection of multiple identities and experiences, addressing the unique needs of individuals who belong to multiple underprivileged groups.

Intersectionality: A concept recognizing that individuals can belong to multiple underprivileged or marginalized groups simultaneously (e.g., a woman of color), and that their experiences are shaped by the intersection of these identities.

Mentorship Programs: Initiatives that connect underprivileged students with mentors from the tech industry or academia, offering guidance, inspiration, and career opportunities.

Microaggressions: Subtle, often unintentional, acts or comments that convey bias or discrimination toward individuals based on their background or identity.

Neurodiversity: Recognizing and valuing neurological differences in individuals, including those with conditions such as autism, ADHD, and dyslexia, as a form of diversity in the tech industry.

Representation Matters: A phrase emphasizing the importance of diverse representation in media, education, and the tech industry to inspire and empower underprivileged individuals.

Role Modeling: Setting an example through one's own behavior, attitudes, and actions to inspire and encourage diversity and inclusion in computer science.

Scholarships and Financial Aid: Financial support programs designed to make computer science education more affordable and accessible to underprivileged students pursuing higher education in the field.

Socioeconomic Mobility: The potential for underprivileged students to improve their economic circumstances and social status through access to quality computer science education and related career opportunities.

STEAM Education: An extension of STEM education that includes the Arts (A), recognizing the importance of creativity and artistic expression in technology and innovation.

STEM Ambassadors: Professionals from science, technology, engineering, and mathematics fields who engage with underprivileged students to inspire and encourage their interest in STEM disciplines.

STEM Diversity: The goal of achieving diversity and inclusion within the fields of science, technology, engineering, and mathematics, including computer science.

STEM Education: An acronym for science, technology, engineering, and mathematics education, which encompasses computer science and related fields and is essential for underprivileged students to access career opportunities in the tech industry.

Systemic Bias: Discriminatory practices or biases that are ingrained in systems, institutions, or cultures, often leading to unequal opportunities for underrepresented groups.

Tech Apprenticeships: Programs that offer on-the-job training and work experience in the tech industry, often targeting individuals from underprivileged backgrounds as a pathway to employment.

Tech Bootcamps: Short-term, intensive training programs that teach practical tech skills, often used by individuals seeking to transition into tech careers.

Tech Bridge Programs: Partnerships between educational institutions, tech companies, and community organizations aimed at bridging the gap between education and employment for underprivileged students.

Tech Diversity Conference: Conferences and events focused on diversity and inclusion in the tech industry, featuring speakers, workshops, and discussions on related topics.

Tech Diversity Report: Annual or periodic reports published by tech companies and organizations to disclose data on the demographic composition of their workforce and their diversity and inclusion initiatives.

Tech Ecosystem: The interconnected network of organizations, institutions, and individuals that contribute to the development and advancement of technology, including startups, academic institutions, and industry leaders.

Tech Entrepreneurship: The practice of creating, scaling, and managing technology-driven businesses, often seen as a pathway to economic empowerment and innovation.

Tech Equity Advocacy: Advocacy efforts aimed at reducing disparities in access to technology and tech-related opportunities for underprivileged communities.

Tech Equity Fund: Financial resources allocated to support underprivileged individuals and communities in gaining access to technology, digital resources, and computer science education.

Tech Inclusion Index: A measurement tool used to assess and rank organizations or regions based on their commitment to diversity and inclusion in the tech industry.

Tech Inclusion Pledge: Commitments made by organizations and institutions to actively work toward increasing diversity and inclusion in the tech industry and education.

Tech Inclusion Pledge: Commitments made by tech companies and organizations to foster diversity and inclusion within their workforce and products.

Tech Industry: The sector of the economy that encompasses technology-related companies, including software development, hardware manufacturing, and digital services.

Tech Literacy Programs: Initiatives that aim to improve the digital literacy of underprivileged individuals by teaching them essential technology skills, including computer use, software applications, and online safety.

Tech Pipeline Programs: Initiatives and educational pathways that aim to increase the number of underprivileged students pursuing computer science and tech-related degrees and careers.

Unconscious Bias Training: Workshops and programs designed to raise awareness of and mitigate implicit biases among educators, policymakers, and professionals.

Underprivileged Groups: Individuals and communities who face economic, social, or educational disadvantages, often resulting from poverty, lack of access to resources, or systemic inequalities.

Underrepresented Students: Individuals from demographic groups that are historically and currently underrepresented in computer science and related fields, such as women, people of color, and those with disabilities.

Universal Design for Learning (UDL): An educational framework that emphasizes designing learning experiences and materials that accommodate the diverse needs and preferences of all students, including those with disabilities and from underprivileged backgrounds.

References

Abdul Kalam, A. P. J. (n.d.). *A. P. J. Abdul Kalam quotes.* Lib Quotes. https://libquotes.com/a-p-j-abdul-kalam/quote/lbk7n1u

ACCESS. (2015, May 1). *About.* https://access-ca.org/about

Alvarado, E. (2022, July 19). *Language quotes to motivate and inspire learners.* Spanish Mama. https://spanishmama.com/language-quotes-for-language-learners

Andrews, S., and Morris, L. (2020, August 9). Diversity in CS: Race and gender among CS majors in 2015 vs 2020. *The Stanford Daily.* https://stanforddaily.com/2020/08/08/how-has-diversity-within-stanfords-cs-department-changed-over-the-past-5-years

Bailey, S. (2022, August 15). *AP classes: Are they worth it?* BestColleges. https://www.bestcolleges.com/blog/ap-classes-are-they-worth-it

BestColleges. (2022, July 1). *Scholarships for computer science.* BestColleges. https://www.bestcolleges.com/computer-science/computer-science-scholarships

Brookes Publishing. (2023, July 8). *Quote.* https://twitter.com/BrookesPubCo/status/1412894956939788295

Bryant, K. (2017, April 14). *Inspirational Quotes at BrainyQuote.* BrainyQuotes. https://www.brainyquote.com/quotes/kimberly_bryant_895247

Carlton, G. (2022, November 8). *Resource guide for Hispanic and Latino/a students in STEM.* BestColleges. https://www.bestcolleges.com/resource/hispanic-latino-students-in-stem

Cherokee Nation. (2021, January 4). MotivationMonday. Facebook. https://www.facebook.com/TheCherokeeNation/photos/a.125970577528729/3482974765161610/?type=3

Code.org. (n.d.). *Native American and Indigenous Peoples initiative.* Code.org. https://code.org/naipi

Cowell, A. (2019, June 5). Overlooked no more: Alan Turing, condemned code breaker and computer visionary. *New York Times.*

https://www.nytimes.com/2019/06/05/obituaries/alan-turing-overlooked.html

Department for Education. (2016, October 20). *National curriculum in England: Computing programmes of study.* gov.uk. https://www.gov.uk/government/publications/national-curriculum-in-england-computing-programmes-of-study/national-curriculum-in-england-computing-programmes-of-study#key-stage-4

Dodge, A. (2019, November 7). *How to incorporate STEAM learning in lessons about Native American culture.* Ozobot. https://ozobot.com/how-to-incorporate-steam-learning-in-lessons-about-native-american-culture

Domagala, D. (n.d.). *English for IT - resources.* Fluentbe Knowledge Base. https://intercom.help/fluentbe/en/articles/4233237-english-for-it-resources

Erickson, L. A. (2021, April 29).*9 tips for helping your students become activists. Ed Post.* https://www.edpost.com/stories/9-tips-for-helping-your-students-become-activists

Falasz, B. (2022, July 6). *24 activities to get families involved in schools.* PowerSchool. https://www.powerschool.com/blog/24-activities-to-get-families-involved-in-schools

Fine, C. *(n.d.) Cordelia Fine quotes.* QuoteFancy. https://quotefancy.com/quote/1778029/Cordelia-Fine-Both-women-and-computer-science-are-the-losers-when-a-geeky-stereotype

Harding, X. (2016, August 30). *Coding diversity into Silicon Valley: Our talk with Kimberly Bryant, CEO of Black Girls Code.* Popular Science. https://www.popsci.com/black-girls-code-kimberly-bryant-coding-diversity-into-silicon-valley

Hurst, A. (2022, December 1). *The top reasons why a lack of diversity in tech remains a problem.* Information Age. https://www.information-age.com/why-lack-of-diversity-in-tech-remains-problem-18926

Isaac Computer Science. (2017, March 6). *Isaac Computer Science.* https://isaaccomputerscience.org/glossary?examBoard=all&stage=all

Kumar, M. & Kumar, M. T. (2014, August 25). *Why there aren't more Latinos in the tech industry*. MSNBC. https://www.msnbc.com/jose-diaz-balart/the-latino-tech-imperative-msna398071

Lenharo, M. (2023, July 18). *The true cost of science's language barrier for non-native English speakers*. Nature. https://www.nature.com/articles/d41586-023-02320-2

Lisalisa, L. (2014, May 24). *When schools, families, and community groups work... Inspiring quotes for parent group leaders*. Pinterest. https://www.pinterest.com/pin/549298485773891608

Lombardi, P. (2017, March 16). *21 types of computer science jobs*. Indeed. https://www.indeed.com/career-advice/finding-a-job/types-of-computer-science-jobs

Lovereide, E. (2019, March 3). *Kalwant Bhopal: It pays to be white on campus*. Kifinfo. https://kifinfo.no/en/2018/10/kalwant-bhopal-pays-to-be-white

Lutkevich, B. (2022, October 24). *6 reasons why diversity in STEM is important*. TechTarget. https://www.techtarget.com/whatis/feature/Reasons-why-diversity-in-STEM-is-important

Marken, S. & Crabtree, S., (2021, October 5). *Role models spark students' interest in computer science*. Gallup. https://news.gallup.com/poll/355070/role-models-spark-students-interest-computer-science.aspx

Owens, P.H. (2020, October 2). *Voices of diversity: Standing up to bigotry and discrimination*. Detroit Regional Chamber. https://www.detroitchamber.com/voices-of-diversity-standing-up-to-bigotry-and-discrimination

Pelser, R. (2020, July 10). *Leadership for change*. OAPEN Home. https://library.oapen.org/bitstream/id/62fa78f0-d7df-4af1-871a-3b11d949a47c/9781928523901.pdf

Post, K. (2023, September 19). *Why high school students should take AP computer science*. Noble Desktop. https://www.nobledesktop.com/classes-near-me/blog/why-high-school-students-should-take-ap-computer-science

P-TECH. (2018, August 10). *Learn about P-TECH schools*. P-TECH. https://www.ptech.org/about

Thompson, H. (2022, April 26). *Introducing kids to positive role models*. Safe Search Kids. https://www.safesearchkids.com/introducing-your-kids-to-positive-role-models

Wani, B. (2022, January 24). *Why we need diversity curriculum in schools?* Ground Report. https://groundreport.in/why-we-need-diversity-curriculum-in-schools

Washington, A. N. (2016, June 10). *Where are the computer science role models for students of color?* Tumblr. https://teacherblog.code.org/post/145716241244/where-are-the-computer-science-role-models-for

Women of Silicon Valley. (2017, November 29). *Just 18 really awesome native folks in STEM*. Medium. https://medium.com/women-of-silicon-valley/just-18-awesome-native-folks-in-stem-134211ff14cd